D0065341

Nielsen

Category Management

Positioning Your
Organization to Win

Published by NTC Business
Books in Association with Nielsen
Marketing Research and the
American Marketing Association

AMERICAN
MARKETING
ASSOCIATION

NTC Business Books
a division of *NTC Publishing Group*

Cataloging-in-Publication information is available from the Library of Congress.

Published by NTC Business Books, a division of NTC Publishing Group
4255 West Touhy Avenue, Lincolnwood (Chicago), Illinois 60646-1975, U.S.A.

Published in conjunction with:
Nielsen Marketing Research, Nielsen Plaza, Northbrook, Illinois 60062, and
The American Marketing Association, 250 South Wacker Drive, Chicago, Illinois 60606.

While every effort has been made in the preparation of this book to ensure accuracy of the statistical and other contents, the publisher and data suppliers cannot accept any liability in respect of errors or omissions, or for any costs, losses, consequential damages or any other damages arising from such errors or omissions. Readers will appreciate that the data and other contents are only as up-to-date as their availability and compilation and printing schedules will allow, and are subject to change during the natural course of events. Hence, any events arising after March 1992 have not been accounted for and while the data contents are the latest available at the relevant time for compilation during 1992 we cannot guarantee their accuracy.

Acknowledgements

The task of gathering and analyzing the data contained in the Nielsen Category Management Book required contributions from all parts of the Nielsen Marketing Research Company. We would like to thank all those who have contributed to the preparation of the Category Management Book.

Nielsen Marketing Research
Nielsen Retail Information Group
Nielsen Household Services
Nielsen Creative Services

Trademarks

NIELSEN,® SCANTRACK,® HBA,® SPACEMAN,® CONQUEST,® NIELSEN SPOTLIGHT,® PROCISION,® NIELSEN SALES ADVISOR,® ClusterPLUS,® and SCAN✳FACT® PC are registered trademarks of A.C. Nielsen Company.

ScorPLUS,™ and ASTRO-SET ™ are trademarks of A.C. Nielsen Company.

Manufactured in the United States of America.

3 4 5 6 7 8 9 0 VP 9 8 7 6 5 4 3 2 1

PREFACE

These are challenging times for manufacturers and retailers in the consumer packaged goods marketplace. Competition is stiffer than ever. Consumers have never been more sophisticated. And distribution channels are blurring as the marketplace becomes increasingly fragmented.

The uncertainties and competitive challenges caused by these forces are affecting all marketers as they strive to survive and succeed in the unpredictable 1990s.

But just as tremendous heat and pressure create a diamond, today's tough marketplace has produced a valuable new marketing idea that offers a wealth of opportunity for those who can mine and polish its potential.

Known as category management, this innovative idea has already been adopted by several major companies, and many others are planning to do the same.

As the world's leading marketing research company, Nielsen Marketing Research has played a significant role in the rapid evolution of category management as a powerful marketing tool.

Working with manufacturers and retailers, Nielsen has developed a wide range of software-based analytical products that are enabling our clients to implement category management successfully. These tools allow our clients to harness the power of market data and to channel it into customized marketing strategies.

We also have developed a practical understanding of the "dos and don'ts" of category management. We have had the unique opportunity to view it from the perspective of the manufacturer *and* the retailer. And although it involves similar steps and goals for both, we have learned that many important differences exist.

Recognizing these nuances, as well as the growing importance of category management in today's marketplace, Nielsen has distilled its category management knowledge into this "how-to" style handbook. Its purpose is to help our customers and others gain a detailed understanding of how category management works, so they can benefit fully from this exciting new concept.

Category management is clearly the wave of the future in the consumer packaged goods marketplace. By reading and studying the pages that follow, you can catch the wave—and ride it to future success.

John H. Costello

John H. Costello
President & COO
NMR USA

FOREWORD

• •

While category management is not a new idea for retailers or manufacturers, successfully using it to manage your business more profitably is. As the world's leading marketing research company, Nielsen undertook the challenge to develop a theoretical and practical category management strategy. The result, this book, is a basic blueprint for implementing category management by manufacturers and retailers. Because it is a generic blueprint, it can be customized to help your business move into this new and exciting arena.

This book was compiled by people who have years of experience in the manufacturing, retailing, and market research industries. They squeezed time out of already full schedules to bring category management to life in a meaningful, practical way.

Karl Gnau, vice president, sales management services, articulated the manufacturer's point of view focusing on sales force needs.

Tom Richardson, vice president, retail applications manager, developed the retailer's strategy concentrating on pricing issues.

Jim Dippold, vice president, product development, drove the book with his vision of category management—based on his extensive retail background, product planning and space management experience.

Greg Starzynski, vice president, director of marketing, Nielsen Household Services, was the consumer expert responsible for the consumer research, advertising response models, and consumer targeting pieces.

Ken Wisniewski, Ph.D., vice president, director of advanced analytic technologies, was the expert on promotion modeling.

Allan Rau, industry account manager, packaged goods, drew on his knowledge of lifestyle clusters to act as the project's consumer targeting professional.

Connie Latson, marketing communications specialist, developed the case study strategy and managed the information flow and editorial changes.

Sandy Rebitzer, director of marketing communications & advertising, drove the entire process.

To all of you and to the countless others who strategized, produced and analyzed data, thank you. And to all of you who read it, may it help you navigate through your own category management process.

David Lonsdale
President
Nielsen Software & Systems

Rudolph (Doss) Struse
Sr. Vice President
Nielsen Marketing Research

Paul J.J. Payack
Vice President
Corporate Communications
Nielsen Marketing Research

TABLE OF CONTENTS

INTRODUCTION

**Speaking
Categorically:
Managing Your
Business in
the 1990s**

• • • • • • • • • • • • • •

Sometimes a marketing idea comes along that is perfectly in tune with its time. It addresses an important need, dovetails with new technology, and promises to improve the bottom line.

Soon, it becomes a standard way of doing business.

The challenge for manufacturers and retailers, of course, is identifying the idea, recognizing its potential, and taking advantage of it before the competition does.

Back in the heyday of mass marketing in the 1950s, TV advertising was this kind of idea. It enabled marketers to reach a huge audience, capitalized on new technology, and promised to increase sales and profits.

Soon, everybody was using it.

Today, manufacturers and retailers competing in a new era are beginning to recognize the long-term potential of another fledgling marketing idea.

Information
⋮
| Technology |
⋮
| Software Applications |
⋮
⋮

Category Management

The Era of Category Management

It's called "category management," and it reflects the changes that have made the consumer packaged goods marketplace of the 1990s more complex than ever.

Just as TV advertising enabled marketers of the 1950s to deliver their product messages to large numbers of people, category management allows retailers and manufacturers today to aim their products at market niches. This micromarketing is not possible without category management.

Just as TV advertising took advantage of the growing popularity of a new technology, category manage-

8

ment capitalizes on the dramatic increase in market information, advances in technology, and sophisticated software applications.

And just as TV advertising promised to increase sales and profits, category management provides a way to enhance margins now squeezed by intense competition in a marketplace replete with shopping options.

What exactly *is* category management?

Boiled down to basics, category management is a process that involves managing product categories as business units and customizing them on a store-by-store basis to satisfy customer needs.

Rooted in the belief that today's new-product explosion has made strategic management by item too impractical and strategic management by department too unfocused, category management transforms retail "buyers" and manufacturer "sellers" into entrepreneurs, each responsible for a small business within a larger enterprise.

"Category management empowers an individual within a company to operate a category like a business," says Ronald Ziegler, president and chief executive officer of the National Association of Chain Drug Stores. "Through this process, you can identify the optimal product mix and stock each store with the specific products that demographics indicate customers wish to purchase."

Although category management produces merchandising programs tailored to individual stores, its ultimate goal is to unite these programs to support a company's mission, image and strategic objectives.

Before implementing category management, retailers and manufacturers must define their mission/image and develop marketing strategies

Boiled down to basics, category management is a process that involves managing product categories as business units and customizing them on a store-by-store basis to satisfy customer needs.

Speaking Categorically:
Managing Your Business in the 1990s

and objectives to further it. In doing so, they must determine what role individual product categories will be expected to play in their corporate game plan, beginning with a clear definition of each category.

Retailers and manufacturers also must begin to look at themselves—and each other—in a much different way. They must redesign their organizations, integrating functions and responsibilities to create entrepreneurial "category managers." In addition, retailers and manufacturers must push aside adversarial feelings to develop mutually beneficial strategic alliances based on sharing market intelligence.

Changing Roles

Old Roles

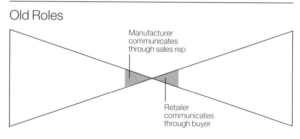

New Roles

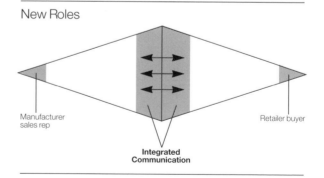

Thinking "Inside the Circle"

Retailers and manufacturers who understand and share a commitment to the tools of information, technology and applications can realize fully the benefits of category management.

For example, category management requires continual evaluation of sales and demographic data to determine who buys what in a particular category, where they buy it, how often, and how much they spend. Information, technology and applications can help you answer these questions, as well as many others. You can identify brand-loyal consumers and high-volume shoppers, pinpoint their media preferences, and gauge their responsiveness to specific promotions. You also can determine how the performance of one category affects other categories in the same store.

Armed with these data, you can develop customized strategies for individual categories in specific stores—based on a retailer's image, a category's strategic role, and a store's location and customer demographics. Specifically, you can tailor category assortments, shelf-space allocations, pricing, and consumer and trade promotions to maximize sales and profits. Best of all, you can test such strategies before implementing them by using sophisticated computer modeling programs.

By capitalizing on information, technology and applications, category management enables you to provide customers with the products they want, when they want them—at competitive prices.

Speaking Categorically: Managing Your Business in the 1990s

It's important to remember that category management is a circular, long-term process, not a linear, short-term project. It involves five ongoing stages, each of which flows naturally into the next, allowing retailers and manufacturers to adapt quickly to marketplace changes. The stages include:

1. Reviewing the category
2. Targeting consumers
3. Planning merchandising
4. Implementing strategy
5. Evaluating results

Although the general concepts behind each stage are the same for retailers and manufacturers, there are significant differences in execution and logistics. In addition, numerous opportunities exist for retailers and manufacturers to help each other to implement category management successfully. It's possible to practice category management without such interaction, but the process works best when retailers and manufacturers recognize the need to market together and share their powerful marketing capabilities. This type of strategic alliance improves the retailer's ability to build his image and to offer customized product assortments, merchandising and promotions; enhances the manufacturer's ability to build brand image and equity; and bolsters both parties' ability to respond effectively to customer needs.

What's Ahead

Separate chapters later in this book focus on category management for retailers and category management for manufacturers. Each chapter includes an example of category management in action. A concluding chapter discusses retailer-manufacturer synergies created by category management, and the likely long-term impact of category management on consumer packaged goods marketing.

Before examining these areas, though, let's take a closer look at the marketplace trends that are making category management an ideal marketing concept for the 1990s and beyond.

CHAPTER

· ·

Changing Market-
place Requires
Changing Strategy

Changing Marketplace Requires Changing Strategy

• • • • • • • • • • • • • • • • •

During the last 20 years, two major trends have reshaped the consumer packaged goods marketplace. One is marketplace fragmentation; the other is the growth of technology, applications and information.

Demographic and lifestyle changes have caused marketplace fragmentation, creating a kaleido-scope of images that contrasts sharply with the homogeneity of the 1950s.

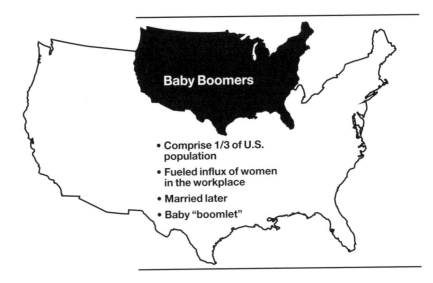

Baby Boomers

- **Comprise 1/3 of U.S. population**
- **Fueled influx of women in the workplace**
- **Married later**
- **Baby "boomlet"**

The 78-million-strong Baby Boom generation, born between 1946 and 1964, has driven many of the lifestyle changes that have led to fragmentation. The Baby Boomers, who comprise about one-third of the U.S. population, have fueled the influx of women into the workplace, have married later than previous generations, and have touched off a "Baby Boomlet" as they have become parents.

The middle-aging of the Baby Boomers and increased life expectancies for all Americans have led to an overall aging of the U.S. population, a phenomenon known as the "Graying of America." In 1990, the nation's median age jumped to its highest level ever—32.8, up from 30 in 1980. And by the year 2020, people over 65 will account for 20 percent of the population, compared with 13 percent today, according to the Census Bureau.

These trends, coupled with the nation's economic woes in the early 1990s, including a long-term decline in real (after-inflation) wages, have produced a dizzying array of household types. The nation's expanding ethnic population, meanwhile, has added to the growing diversity of American lifestyles.

Together, these trends have lowered the boom on the consumer packaged goods marketplace, shattering it into numerous fragments, each with its own tastes, needs and values that marketers must attempt to discern.

A few common denominators do exist among today's consumers. Lifestyle changes, for example, have left little time for shopping in many households, triggering widespread demand for convenience and service. In this environment, one-stop shopping and time-saving products hold great appeal. Also, the ranks of savvy, experienced shoppers are expanding as the population ages. Worried about economic uncertainties and their own growing financial obligations, middle-aging Baby Boomers are demanding quality and value for their hard-earned dollars—and they're not alone.

The challenge of answering these broad-based demands, while addressing the needs of specific niches, has made marketing more complex than

Chapter 1

Changing Marketplace Requires Changing Strategy

• • • • • • • • • • • • • • • •

ever. Complicating matters further, fragmentation in the consumer marketplace has been accompanied by a proliferation of retail store formats, a blurring of the lines between retail trade channels, and media fragmentation.

1.1 Store Characteristics by Format

Typical Store Averages—1990

	Total Area (Sq. Ft.)	Weekly Sales	# of Items	GM/HBC % of Sales
Conventional Supermarket	22,500	$138,000	15,000	8%
Superstore	42,000	$290,000	23,000	13%
Food/Drug Combo	54,000	$375,000	29,000	18%
Super Combo	95,000	$950,000	60,000+	35%
Warehouse Store	43,000	$215,000	14,500	6%
Super Warehouse	59,000	$555,000	22,500	8%
Hypermarket	174,000	$1,440,000	100,000+	40%
Limited Assortment	10,000	$61,000	800	6%
Wholesale Club	105,000	$970,000	5,000	65%
Convenience Store (Traditional)	2,500	$11,300*	3,400	7%
Convenience Store (Petroleum-based)	1,900	$8,900*	2,300	8%
Other	N/A	$18,500	N/A	N/A

Source: Willard Bishop Consulting, Ltd., *Competitive Edge*, May 1991
*Merchandise sales only (non-gas).

Attracting Customers Is Tougher Than Ever

The number of retail store formats has literally exploded. Consider, for example, segmentation occurring within the four primary types of retail outlets—food stores, chain drug stores, mass merchandisers and wholesale clubs. A recent survey compares 11 different formats within these outlets alone (see chart 1.1). Retail organizations are developing superstores, discount stores and ethnic outlets. Many outlets, including superstores, super combos, wholesale clubs, discount drug stores and warehouse stores, are expected to continue to increase their market penetration significantly.

The lines between traditional retail trade channels are blurring further as retailers scramble to offer the convenience of one-stop shopping. Food stores are expanding into mass merchandise; mass merchandisers are expanding into food; and drug stores are expanding into mass merchandise and food. With competition intensifying among retailers, attracting consumers to particular stores and brands has become increasingly difficult. Faced with a plethora of shopping choices, today's savvy shoppers often view retailers as interchangeable— and that has made consumer behavior less predictable than ever.

Despite the general demand for one-stop shopping, research shows that certain consumers will buy certain products from specific stores. This finding reflects the fact that shoppers have been conditioned to look for deals in certain categories and often select retail outlets based on the availability of such deals. It's not uncommon, for example, to find the same consumer shopping both high-end and low-end outlets, saving money on certain items in order to better afford luxury items.

This trend has increased pressure on retailers to differentiate themselves by developing a reputation as the place to shop for certain product categories. When done successfully, differentiation along these lines can infuse a retailer's name with brand equity, establishing a clear connection in consumers' minds between the name and the fulfillment of certain needs.

Reaching consumers with any type of marketing message, however, has become increasingly difficult because of the fragmentation of traditional media. Network TV, home to the mass-market ads of the 1950s, no longer rules the TV roost, as cable TV channels have exploded in number, capturing both viewers and advertising dollars. VCRs and remote-

Chapter 1

Changing Marketplace Requires Changing Strategy

• • • • • • • • • • • • • •

Two-thirds of today's brand-selection decisions are made in the store.

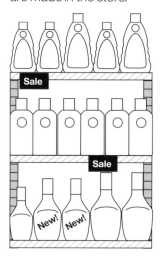

control devices, along with the emergence of pay-per-view programming, have muddied the TV advertising waters even further. The fragmentation trend also has hit other traditional advertising media, including newspapers, magazines and radio stations.

Reflecting these changes and the hectic pace of modern lifestyles, two-thirds of today's brand-selection decisions are made in the store, consumer research shows. Manufacturers consequently are focusing greater attention on understanding consumers and tailoring in-store marketing and merchandising to meet their needs. Spending on trade and consumer promotions has grown dramatically in recent years, with more and more manufacturers considering non-traditional ways of getting their message across to consumers as part of an overall effort to leverage brands through retailers.

Research Advances Keep Targeted Consumers in Sight

Fortunately, advances in technology, applications and information have kept pace with the changing consumer packaged goods marketplace, enabling manufacturers and retailers to develop an understanding of consumers' diverse needs and purchasing habits.

There has been a burgeoning growth in the collection, analysis and quality of market data. New technology has made it more practical to collect a wider breadth of information on a more timely basis, paving the way for more knowledgeable marketing and merchandising decision-making.

At the same time, manufacturers and retailers can identify the demographic, socioeconomic and lifestyle characteristics of consumers down to the level of city blocks. Market research services are increasing market intelligence further by generating detailed reports on the purchase behavior of American households. These data, coupled with scanning data, can produce detailed profiles of neighborhood purchase patterns. The computerized capability to analyze scanning data with causal data on advertising and promotions and consumer research provides additional information about purchase behavior on the national, regional and local levels.

Computer software advancements also are allowing marketers to forecast, monitor and quickly adjust the optimal product mix, shelf-space allocation, pricing, and promotions for specific categories at individual stores. This capability is helping marketers develop, implement and evaluate customized merchandising strategies for individual stores.

To make sense out of the growing amount of market data now available, retailers and manufacturers have been relying increasingly on information research companies to help them gain a competitive advantage and to implement efficient strategies such as category management.

Relationships Between Retailers and Manufacturers Change

Advances in technology, applications and information not only have helped retailers to understand their customers better, but also have given them greater power in their dealings with manufacturers. Striving to increase profits by reducing costs, they're using scanning data to become more category-focused, to make smarter buying decisions, and to fuel electronic inventory management systems that allow

Chapter 1

Changing Marketplace Requires Changing Strategy

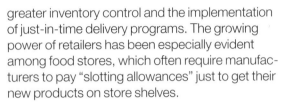

Manufacturers and retailers today must see clearly at all levels of the marketplace, including the traditional national and market levels, as well as the total-chain and individual-store levels.

greater inventory control and the implementation of just-in-time delivery programs. The growing power of retailers has been especially evident among food stores, which often require manufacturers to pay "slotting allowances" just to get their new products on store shelves.

The growth in retailers' power has coincided with manufacturers' increasing need to focus on local markets. Traditionally, manufacturers, like national retailers, have been concerned primarily with building brand equity nationally. But marketplace and media fragmentation have created a new challenge: balancing national brand-building efforts with local ones.

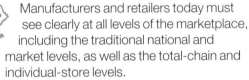

Manufacturers and retailers today must see clearly at all levels of the marketplace, including the traditional national and market levels, as well as the total-chain and individual-store levels.

With category-focused retailers making purchase decisions based on the strength an item brings to a category, manufacturers must provide retailers with category-related information, not just brand perspectives. Does a brand fill out a product line? Does it satisfy a market niche?

Manufacturers also must use fact-based selling to demonstrate that an item will increase category sales and not just take sales away from other products in the category. Advances in technology, applications and information are giving manufacturers the tools they need to make such presentations.

Category information establishes an ongoing dialogue between the retailer and the manufacturer. By sharing marketing information, they can assess each other's needs better and form a mutually beneficial strategic alliance. Both can take advantage of technology to monitor trends and profitability. They then can direct their advertising and trade promotion dollars more wisely, while keeping in mind the profit margin on a product or category. Each party can advocate a marketing position and cooperate to the most effective degree possible while meeting its own strategic goals.

Although advances in technology, applications and information have given retailers and manufacturers new tools to decipher the increasingly complex consumer products marketplace, they haven't provided all the answers, nor have they magically distributed market intelligence equally. Manufacturers still know things that retailers don't know, and vice versa. By pooling their resources, both parties can gain market knowledge they can't obtain by themselves. More and more retailers and manufacturers are recognizing this fact as the use of information and technology becomes more widespread and pressure increases for everyone to make accurate marketing decisions more quickly.

Category Management Model Is the Marketing Vehicle for Driving Business

The fragmentation of the consumer packaged goods marketplace and the growing use of technology, applications and information by retailers and manufacturers have created a fertile environment for the implementation of category management.

Both retailers and manufacturers are seeking new strategies for increasing sales and profits in today's fragmented, intensely competitive marketplace. Retailers are searching for new ways to attract and retain savvy customers, and manufacturers are looking for new ways to reach market niches with their product messages and to sell retailers on their

Changing Marketplace Requires Changing Strategy

• • • • • • • • • • • • • • • •

brands. Both parties are recognizing the need to work together to capitalize fully on the potential of information technology.

In the face of these pressing needs, the old way of doing business—in which retailers assigned individual "buyers" to deal only with individual manufacturers, and manufacturers' "reps" worried only about taking orders—has become obsolete.

The changing marketplace is demanding strategic changes by retailers and manufacturers so they can improve their understanding of today's consumers and align product categories with their diversified needs.

Category management enables retailers and manufacturers to accomplish these objectives, while also improving sales and profitability. The process addresses marketplace fragmentation head-on, and runs on the fuel of technology, applications and information. It is truly a marketing vehicle for its time.

CHAPTER

2

Retailers Checking
Out New Ways to Do
Business

Retailers Checking Out New Ways to Do Business

In the early to mid-1900s, retailing in the United States was an up-close and personal business.

Americans shopped at local general stores, butcher shops, pharmacies, bakeries, grocery stores, and fruit and vegetable stands, and customers and merchants often knew each other well.

They commonly lived in the same neighborhood, saw each other regularly, and spoke over the counter on a first-name basis, discussing their families, their friends, and issues of the day.

This familiarity—along with the fact that shopkeepers typically took and filled each shopper's total order—made retailers very knowledgeable about their customers' tastes and needs.

Using this knowledge, they tailored their merchandise and promotions for their neighborhood, and their customers rewarded them with shopping loyalty.

Today, retailers are rediscovering this success formula in a consumer packaged goods marketplace that bears little apparent resemblance to those simple days of yesteryear.

They're doing so through the process of category management, which involves managing product categories as individual business units and customizing them according to customer preference within stores.

Retailers practicing category management use information and technology to listen to their customers in much the same way their predecessors took advantage of the neighborhood grapevine and over-the-counter chats with customers. Using electronic checkout scanners, computerized programs that provide local demographic profiles, computer databases that track consumer purchase behavior, and software programs that integrate sales data with pricing, promotion, merchandising, and consumer data, retailers are learning as much—and sometimes more—about their customers as the shopkeepers of the early 1900s knew about theirs.

Retailers of the 1990s that have implemented category management are using their growing customer knowledge to develop customized merchandising and marketing programs for individual categories, all geared toward the tastes and needs of target customers.

In this way, category management is bringing retailers full circle, putting them back in touch with their customer roots after years of serving as the mass-market distribution arm of manufacturers.

Today's category managers are the new shopkeepers of retailing, each an entrepreneur responsible for the success—or failure—of a small business.

Category Managers

Entrepreneur 1   **Entrepreneur 2**   **Entrepreneur 3**

More Retailers Catching Latest Wave of Category Management

Some retailers with corporate cultures that encourage entrepreneurial empowerment have practiced category management for years. With the increased use of information, scanners and other technology among retailers of all types, a growing number of other retailers now are recognizing the benefits of

Retailers Checking Out New Ways to Do Business

• • • • • • • • • • • • • • • • •

category management and are implementing it to maximize sales and profits. There are three driving forces behind this trend.

The first is that demographic and socioeconomic trends have fragmented the consumer packaged goods marketplace into countless segments, just as immigration divided American cities of the early 1900s into a variety of highly diverse neighborhoods.

Like old-time shopkeepers, retailers are striving to match their stores' form to customer needs, which has led to a proliferation of store formats.

Shoppers of the 1990s are highly mobile, and faced with a dizzying array of shopping options, they can be highly fickle, cherry-picking among retailers based on how they measure up in terms of price, quality, convenience and service.

With a variety of stores offering similar products, retailers have become largely interchangeable in consumers' minds, and individual retailers must work harder than ever to differentiate themselves from the pack. You must establish an identity as the place that provides a particular shopping experience, and in the process, you must strive to make your name a brand name.

"The key to responding effectively to the demographic shifts going on throughout the country is to localize merchandise for the stores," says the president of one leading retail organization. "It's surprising how in some communities, even the basic things are really different."

The second major reason for the growing popularity of category management is the new-product explosion of recent years. It has created a need for a scientific method through which retailers can allocate limited amounts of shelf space and can determine the optimal product mix for a particular store.

With the proliferation of new products, strategic management by department level has become too unfocused, and strategic management by item has become too impractical. Category management gives retailers a manageable, effective way to sort through the new-product explosion to determine which offerings and deals best serve their customers in specific categories, and best support their company's overall mission, image, and objectives.

When implemented successfully, category management enables a retailer to develop a clear identity. In a marketplace bombarded with stores and new products, it enables the retailer to stand out from the crowd.

The third force behind the trend toward category management is the fact that retailers have already increased profits through tightened inventory control and buying practices, such as forward-buying and slotting allowances. As competition intensifies, they now are looking for other ways to improve profits, and they're focusing on selling practices, including improved merchandising and promotions.

As they do so, they increasingly are concluding that when you're up against stiff competition in a highly fragmented marketplace, and the other guys are using information technology and category management, you must do the same if you want to survive and prosper.

Product explosion has created a need for a scientific method through which retailers can allocate limited amounts of shelf space and can determine the optimal product mix for a particular store.

Chapter 2
Retailers Checking Out New Ways to Do Business

Retailers Can Profit from Category Management

What are the specific benefits of category management?

First and foremost, the process heightens your awareness of consumer needs and brings a consumer-oriented focus to your business strategies. In essence, category management allows you to "micro-merchandise" by managing your business based on the way people shop it. When you practice category management, you use consumer preference as your guide when dealing with important issues such as:

- What items to carry,
- In what quantities,
- At what prices,
- At what stores,
- With what shelf space,
- With what promotions, and
- At what locations in the store.

At the same time, category management improves asset management by enabling you to manage your product mix, shelf space, inventory, and capital more effectively.

Category management improves decision-making and allows you to respond quickly to unexpected changes in the marketplace, whether they affect an entire category or subcategory, a specific store, or specific items within a store. Rather than making isolated brand decisions, you can make decisions about brands to meet category goals.

Employing category management also improves your ability to assess the impact of advertising and

30

promotions and to modify them as necessary. You can more readily identify and capitalize on cross-merchandising and cross-promotional opportunities between categories, such as beverages and snack foods.

These advantages, coupled with the customer-focused nature of category management, help to improve category sales and profits. In addition, category management helps you to maximize your return on your information and technology investment by providing a framework for combining and interpreting the abundant sales and demographic data now available to you.

Category management requires internal synergies, such as providing coordination between purchasing and merchandising functions; which fosters a positive, entrepreneurial spirit within your company by empowering individual category managers, leading to improved and mutually beneficial relationships with manufacturers, many of whom also are implementing category management. It also increases the likelihood of achieving overall goals because all decisions are made based on their impact and contribution to those goals.

Together, these benefits give you an important competitive advantage in today's increasingly competitive marketplace. They coalesce to align your business with customer needs, to differentiate it from competitors, to improve internal management and coordination, and to increase sales and profits.

A Competitive Advantage with Category Management

- **Align your business with customer needs**
- **Differentiate from competitors**
- **Improve internal management and coordination**
- **Increase sales and profit**

Retailers Checking Out New Ways to Do Business

• • • • • • • • • • • • • • • •

Category Management's Foundation Starts at the Top

How do you build category management into your business?

Unlike a typical construction project, you start at the top. Before you can think about managing individual product categories, you must know who you are as a company. You must define your mission and determine the public image you desire. Are you a high/low, promotion-driven retailer? Or are you strictly an upscale business? Are you a price leader? Or is your niche everyday low-price?

Develop Company-Wide Strategies

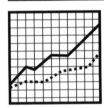

- **Build your image**
- **Develop customer, competitive and supplier positioning**
- **Target your customers**
- **Develop market-share goals**
- **Decide on strategic manufacturer alliances**

Once you nail down your identity, you must develop company-wide marketing strategies and objectives to support your mission and build your image. In doing so, you need to address issues such as customer positioning, competitive positioning and supplier positioning. Who are your target customers? How will you differentiate yourself in the marketplace? How will you build a brand-like image in consumers' minds? What are your market-share goals? With which manufacturers will you form strategic alliances? What will you require of them?

After answering these questions, your next step is to establish company-wide financial goals, including specific targets for sales, profits and return on assets, and time frames in which these objectives must be met.

Your corporate mission/image and marketing strategies and objectives, coupled with your financial plan, provide the framework for category management. A relationship exists between this framework and individual product categories, with the framework dictating category plans and tactics, and category performance supporting the framework. The strength and congruence of this relationship will determine how successful you will be in creating a public image, increasing market share, and improving your bottom line.

Once you have established your framework of corporate philosophies, strategies and objectives, your next challenge will be to determine how each product category will fit into your corporate game plan. Before you can do this, you must define each category, a task that isn't as easy as it might sound. The way you define a category might differ from the way a manufacturer or market research company sees it, and the way your customers perceive it might be something else entirely.

You should collect all of these opinions, but give the most weight to customers' perceptions, which can be determined by analyzing market research data provided by third parties. A good rule of thumb is that products that are substituted for each other should be grouped in the same category.

For example, you might define shampoos and conditioners as one category; a manufacturer might see them as separate categories; and research data indicates that shoppers regularly choose between purchasing a combination shampoo, which includes shampoo and conditioner, and buying shampoo and conditioner separately. The best course of action would be to group all three products in one category, because they all compete for the same customer.

As the definition of each category comes into focus, make sure you identify important subcategories within each category. These smaller product groupings often behave much differently than the rest of a category and can greatly influence its overall performance. If you group all paper products into one category, for instance, you should keep in mind that napkins, toilet paper and paper towels are distinct subcategories, each with its own unique set of merchandising and promotion dynamics.

A good rule of thumb is that products that are substituted for each other should be grouped in the same category.

Retailers Checking Out New Ways to Do Business

• • • • • • • • • • • • • • • •

You must understand the trends that affect each subcategory, how each subcategory affects the category as a whole, and the ripple effect that subcategories might have on other categories.

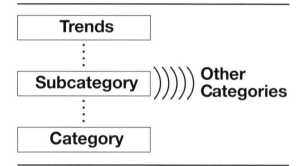

In other words, you must determine what drives each subcategory, how you will take advantage of it, and how you will manage the subcategory in relationship to the category as a whole and other categories within each store.

Another important part of defining a category is taking into account the marketing and logistical considerations for various products.

After you have defined your product categories and have identified key subcategories, you'll be ready to move ahead with the important step of aligning individual categories with your corporate mission/image and overall marketing and financial objectives. Ask yourself what strategic marketing role each category is best suited to play. Is it an image enhancer? A traffic or sales builder? A profit builder?

You can answer these questions by using third-party research data to assess the category's position in your stores versus the marketplace as a whole. How do you fare by category against your competitors? What is your volume? What is your market share? What are your short-term and long-term growth possibilities?

Once you have determined these facts and identified a strategic role for each category, you should establish sales, profit and market-share objectives for each category.

Achieving these goals is the job of the category manager. This headquarters-based person not only serves as the chief buyer for a given category chainwide, but also oversees all sales and merchandising functions within the category. The category manager continually sizes up the marketplace, determines the tactics necessary to meet the category's strategic goals, and ensures that those tactics are carried out.

You can answer these questions by using third-party research data to assess the category's position in your stores versus the marketplace as a whole.

Sound Organizational Structure Is the Cornerstone of Category Management

Before you can designate category managers and delegate authority to them, you must structure your organization to accommodate category management.

Back in the early 20th century, the structure of the typical retail business was simple: The shopkeeper did everything. He dealt with suppliers and customers and determined the product mix, inventory needs, merchandising, promotions and advertising for his store.

This structure became impractical as retail businesses grew larger and retail chains appeared on the scene, leading most retailers to separate

Retailers Checking Out New Ways to Do Business

purchasing from merchandising and to develop specialists in each of these areas (see chart 2.1).

2.1 Traditional Retailer Organization

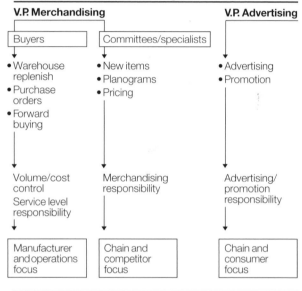

V.P. Merchandising		V.P. Advertising
Buyers	Committees/specialists	
• Warehouse replenish • Purchase orders • Forward buying	• New items • Planograms • Pricing	• Advertising • Promotion
Volume/cost control Service level responsibility	Merchandising responsibility	Advertising/ promotion responsibility
Manufacturer and operations focus	Chain and competitor focus	Chain and consumer focus

In many retailer organizations, buyers typically have been assigned to purchase products by specific manufacturer, not by category, with individual buyers responsible for negotiating all purchase agreements with a particular manufacturer. The buyer traditionally has dealt with a manufacturer's sales rep, who has served basically as an order taker.

Meanwhile, the retailer's buyer and merchandising people, including specialists in pricing, promotions, and shelf-space management, often have worked

separately with manufacturers' marketing and
sales people on issues such as pricing, feature ads,
and displays.

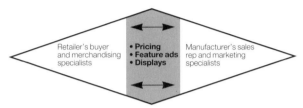

This approach has produced a number of disadvan-
tages, including lack of communication and coordination between purchasing and merchandising.
The buyer, for example, might be responsible for
purchasing detergent from a manufacturer, but
might have no idea about how the product is being
merchandised.

Another disadvantage has been that because
responsibilities are divided among the retailer's
buyer and merchandising people, nobody feels
ultimately responsible for category performance.
As a result, manufacturers sometimes become
confused about who actually is responsible for
making decisions for a retailer.

The most serious disadvantage of this traditional
type of structure is that it hinders a retailer in
developing a unified approach to his product line
and prevents target-specific merchandising. The
retailer does not buy and merchandise products
the way consumers shop for them. With buyers
focused on products and merchandising focused
on volume-boosting tactics, and with each function
accountable to different corporate bosses, assembling a product line becomes a time-consuming,
disjointed process that gets in the way of developing
a consumer-oriented focus and long-term, mutually
beneficial relationships with manufacturers.

Retailers Checking Out New Ways to Do Business

Implementation of category management requires that retailers replace this type of traditional organizational structure with one that integrates category functions and decisions (see chart 2.2).

2.2 Evolving Retailer Organization

V.P. Merchandising		V.P. Marketing

V.P. Merchandising

Director merchandising technology

Category managers
(10-20 categories each)

Analysts
- Data analyses
- Delivery systems
- Space management
- Competitive pricing

Staff support

- Item selections
- Pricing
- Promotions
- Planograms
- Consumer demographics
- Channel competition
- Micro-merchandising

Volume and profit responsibility

Consumer and manufacturer focus

V.P. Marketing

Directors sales and research

- Advertising
- Market intelligence
- Consumer demographics
- Consumer research

Total chain volume and market share responsibility

Chain and consumer focus

There is no single prototype for an ideal organizational structure for category management. If you examine the organizational charts of retailers now practicing category management, you'll discover a number of variations.

One common structure involves four layers of management, including category managers, who report to merchandising managers, who report to a vice president, who reports to the president.

This structure is by no means the dominant one or necessarily the best one for your business. You must determine how many management layers and how many managers you need based on your company's size, mission and corporate culture.

There are two things, however, that are essential to all organizational structures established to implement category management:

1) Buying and merchandising functions, including assortment, pricing, promotion, space management and inventory replenishment, must be integrated under—and managed by—individual category managers.

2) Category managers must be given the freedom and authority to operate their categories like small businesses, developing strategic plans, overseeing their implementation, evaluating their progress, making appropriate adjustments, and being responsible for the results.

The category manager is the opposite of the purchasing and merchandising specialists found in traditional retail organizations. He doesn't specialize, nor is he considered a generalist. You might call the category manager a "totalist," because this person must be a buyer, a merchandiser, a salesman, and a manager—all at the same time. In this way, the category manager is as much an entrepreneur as the shopkeepers of yesteryear were.

Category Manager Profile Shows Different Side of Strategic Planning

What exactly does a category manager do?

His primary task is to develop an annual, chain-wide strategic plan to meet marketing and financial objectives established for the category. This plan must dovetail with the category's strategic role; must reflect the company's mission, image and objectives; and must take into account the company's target consumers and competition.

* * * * * * * * * * * * * * * * * *

Category managers must be given the freedom to operate their categories like small businesses:

- *Developing strategy*
- *Implementing plans*
- *Evaluating progress and making adjustments*
- *Being responsible for results*

Retailers Checking Out New Ways to Do Business

• • • • • • • • • • • • • • •

A category manager may delegate many of the day-to-day tasks, but the success or failure of the category is his responsibility.

In developing this plan, the category manager must determine the maximum product assortment for the stores, and then "target-merchandise" by determining the optimum product mix, inventory levels, shelf-space allocation, pricing, and promotions based on local demographics and customer needs.

Keeping in mind that two-thirds of all brand purchase decisions are made in the store, the category manager also must develop merchandising and promotional tactics to play up his most profitable products and to "close the deal" with shoppers on the spot. For example, the category manager might decide that a high-margin toothpaste should be displayed at eye level so that shoppers would be more likely to purchase it.

As the principal buyer for his category, the category manager must negotiate purchase agreements with multiple manufacturers, hashing out special promotional deals, as well as issues such as payment terms, minimum orders and delivery schedules. He also must enforce company-wide requirements for suppliers. The company, for example, might require that manufacturers:

• Describe the target market for their brands to ensure it is compatible with the retailer's image and target consumers.

• Demonstrate the category-wide impact of merchandising and promoting specific brands.

The category manager also capitalizes on the manufacturer's knowledge of consumer trends, marketplace developments, and category trends to continually refine merchandising and promotion strategies for his category.

Although the category manager sets the strategy and is responsible for the category, he usually doesn't execute all the nitty-gritty tasks associated with these areas. He assigns such duties to a team of specialists. They handle the specifics of shelf-space management, including the creation of planograms and inventory replenishment and delivery logistics. In some cases, a specialist also might handle pricing, working within parameters set by the category manager. But the category manager often decides to handle this area himself. In addition, the category manager decides which items the chain should add, drop, keep, and promote, and then fine-tunes these decisions by store using demographic information.

Delegation of day-to-day tasks does not mean that the category manager shares responsibility for the category with anyone. He has total freedom, authority, and responsibility for all aspects of the category's performance. He ensures that specialists develop effective tactics for executing the strategic plan. If a problem crops up with the category, or if it falls short of its sales and profit objectives, the category manager—not any of his specialists—is accountable.

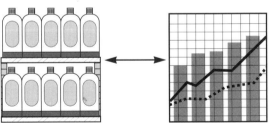

Besides coordinating and over-seeing the activities of the specialists, the category manager must continually compare his category's performance with his plan, by which he will be judged, and make whatever adjustments are necessary. He must be aware of the impact of his category on other categories, and vice versa, and he must identify and capitalize on cross-merchandising and cross-promotional opportunities.

The category manager also must nurture strong relationships with store managers. He must communicate with them frequently and encourage them to relay information about the category's

Retailers Checking Out New Ways to Do Business

• • • • • • • • • • • • • • • •

performance, customers, and the competition. A strong relationship with store managers is critical to a category manager's success, because they play a key role in executing the tactics that support a category's strategic plan. In addition, they often can share market intelligence not revealed by scanning data and other market research. For example, they could tell a category manager whether out-of-stocks had been a problem with a particular promotion, or whether a key competitor had just gone out of business down the block.

Multifaceted Employees May Be Category Manager "Diamonds in the Rough"

Where can you find people with the multifaceted skills and experience necessary to be effective category managers? Fortunately, potential candidates often are within the retailer's own organization.

A category manager must be a totalist, not a specialist. This individual should have purchasing, marketing and merchandising experience, and knowledge of other functions, such as logistics, operations and finance.

Knows:

Marketing

Is:

Purchasing

Totalist

Merchandising

Proactive

Consumer orientation

Category Manager

Multi-tasker

Cross-merchandising

Organized

Technology

Strategic

Logistics

Operations

Finance

Category managers must have a bottom-line consumer orientation, rather than a traditional sales orientation, and they must be proactive in creating demand through their merchandising decisions. To do this, they must be in tune constantly with shoppers' changing attitudes and needs, and must be able to identify growth opportunities and drive consumer demand ahead of the competition, instead of always reacting to the marketplace.

Category managers also must possess strong organizational and people skills. They must be able to handle multiple tasks simultaneously and to deal with a variety of people, ranging from store managers to manufacturers' reps to staff members.

The typical retail chain operation has a deep pool of potential candidates, including buyers, store managers and assistant store managers. As they climb the corporate ladder, these individuals commonly move back and forth between headquarters, regional and store positions, often accumulating the type of "totalist" experience that a category manager needs.

Nonetheless, as you prepare your organization for the shift to category management, make sure to allocate resources to train category managers in strategic thinking and management. Keep in mind that category managers typically handle more than one category, and your company is more likely to benefit from cross-merchandising and cross-promotion synergies between categories when they are managed by the same individual.

You'll also want to make sure that your information and technology capabilities are up to speed: Implementing category management without using scanning equipment in your stores is like trying to sell frozen foods without a freezer.

Category managers must have a bottom-line consumer orientation, rather than a traditional sales orientation, and they must be proactive in creating demand through their merchandising decisions.

Retailers Checking Out New Ways to Do Business

There is one other thing that you shouldn't forget: Restructuring your organization to accommodate category management cannot be done overnight. It is an evolutionary process that can take several years. But that doesn't mean you have to wait that long to implement category management. Once you have made fundamental changes, including the appointment of category managers, implementation of the five stages of category management can begin.

The Five Stages of Category Management

As mentioned earlier, the five stages of category management include:

1. Reviewing the category
2. Targeting consumers
3. Planning merchandising
4. Implementing strategy
5. Evaluating results

None of these stages is a once-only exercise, just as category management is not a linear process. Each stage involves ongoing activities and flows naturally into the next stage, making category management a truly circular process.

The process works best when the category manager relies on an information system that combines internal scanning data with third-party analyses and manufacturers' expertise.

Internal scanning data can provide solid, historical, chainwide statistics on what items were sold, in what quantity, when, where and for what price.

Third-party analyses and manufacturers' expertise can help category managers to determine why products were sold.

Third-party analyses and manufacturers' expertise can help category managers to determine *why* products were sold and to assess the potential of new merchandising and marketing tactics by relating category performance to pricing, promotions, advertising, couponing, competitive activity, demographics, and historical trends within a category. Some of this is data that a retailer *could* develop independently, but most retailers find that dealing with third-party suppliers and manufacturers is more efficient and cost-effective and provides critical information about market performance that the retailer does not have.

Tapping internal and external resources is crucial at every stage of category management, but it is especially so during the category-review stage because it enables the category manager to analyze the history of a category and to answer a host of important questions by measuring a

Reviewing the Category

• • • • • • • • • • • • • • • •

category's performance against the marketplace as a whole. These questions include:

- What is the market share in this category?

- How has the variety/product mix, pricing, promotion, quality, etc., contributed to attaining our market share goals?

- What products are hot? Which aren't?

- Which subcategories are trending up? Which are trending down?

- How are consumer and trade promotions affecting the performance of specific products and the category as a whole?

- How does the category's product mix, pricing, shelf-space allocations, promotions, and location within the store compare with the competition?

◄─────────── **Category** ───────────►

| **Your Store** | Product mix Pricing Shelf-space Promotions Location | **Your Competitor** |

Targeting Consumers

After a category manager has answered these questions, the next challenge is to identify his target customers. The key here is identifying the demographics, lifestyles and purchasing behavior of consumers in the chain's trade area. The category manager gathers data about these consumers' income, education level, occupation, family size, and home ownership, as well as data about what they purchase, where, and how often, and how they respond to promotions.

Consumer databases and software applications programs are available that help the category manager answer countless questions about consumers' purchase behavior, including:

- What type of outlets do they shop at?
- How often do they visit each outlet?
- How much do they spend at each outlet per shopping trip?
- How many items do they buy?
- Are they brand-loyal?
- What sizes do they prefer?
- Are they one-stop convenience shoppers?
- How important is pricing to them?
- How do promotions influence them?
- Do they use coupons?

The answers to these questions allow the category manager to zero in on his target customers—those who account for the greatest percentage of sales and profits in the category.

He also collects media-preference data, which reveal whether certain types of consumers are more likely to receive an advertising message through TV, radio, newspapers or magazines, and which particular stations and publications they prefer.

After gathering all of these data, the category manager then groups stores with similar customer profiles so that he can target each group with customized product assortments, pricing, promotions and shelf-space allocations to meet their needs and to increase store traffic.

Retailers Checking Out New Ways to Do Business

Planning Merchandising

This type of tailoring is what the third stage of category management, planning merchandising, is all about. It involves the creation of a strategic marketing and financial plan for achieving sales and profit goals for the category, based on its strategic role within the company. Technological innovations allow the development and scheduling of customized tactics to carry out the plan.

Computer modeling programs can help the category manager test various pricing, merchandising, and promotion scenarios, and can project whether they will enable him to meet the goals set for the category in areas such as sales volume, profit, market share, and inventory turns.

Price-simulation programs, for example, enable a category manager to develop everyday pricing strategies that will help achieve the category's profit goals and then price individual items to reinforce this plan. Using these programs, category managers can compare their prices—by item and by brand—with those of competitors, and can model various "what-if?" pricing strategies, projecting their impact on product movement and gross margin by item and brand and across the category and comparing those figures with his objectives.

Promotion Planning
Programs

• Price reduction?
• Display?
• Feature ad?
• Coupon?

Promotion planning programs enable a category manager to model the potential effects of promotional deals with manufacturers and identify the right product to promote in order to maximize category profits. These programs integrate historical data and causal details of individual promotions—such as the amount of price reductions, placement of displays, use of feature ads/coupons—as well as data on manufacturers' allowances to show how the promotion might affect the financial performance of a particular brand, the category as a whole and a department. If a category manager, for instance, wanted to promote a 32-ounce size of a particular detergent, he could determine whether the promotion would reduce sales of another brand or would negatively affect only the smaller sizes of the brand being promoted.

A promotion planning program also allows the category manager to make all merchandising and quantity decisions for an entire line of promoted products simply by entering data for a single "master item." In addition, merchandising and operations management can use such programs to review the projected impact of individual promotions by department across an entire chain, and to require modifications in the promotion plan if it appears likely to fall short of sales and gross-margin objectives.

Once a promotion is locked in, a promotion planning program can provide a menu of reports for communications with store and headquarters management. It also can monitor co-op allowances, compare actual results to promotion estimates and maintain a database with information about the details and impact of promotions.

Shelf-space management programs enable the category manager to develop store-specific planograms for individual categories based on a retailer's marketing and merchandising philosophies and operational and financial guidelines, as well as store-level demographics.

Such programs take into account a number of complex variables, such as the size and type of fixturing used in a store; how inventory is ordered, supplied

Shelf-space management programs enable the category manager to develop store-specific planograms for individual categories.

Retailers Checking Out New Ways to Do Business

• • • • • • • • • • • • • • •

Some space-management programs can produce planograms with photographic facsimiles of products displayed on store shelves.

and stocked for the store; replenishment cycles; case-quantity minimums; profitability objectives; service levels; pricing; and space management.

In essence, shelf-space management programs also enable a retailer to optimize category sales and profitability, minimize inventory and maximize merchandising effectiveness by stocking more of the products that appeal to a strategic market trade area, and less of those products that do not appeal to the area.

Some space-management programs can produce planograms with photographic facsimiles of products displayed on store shelves. The space management process also can be automated. Given the proper instructions by a category manager, a space-management program can run around the clock, producing planograms that ensure the right products will be in the right stores in the right quantities at the right time and in the right shelf position. This enhances the category manager's productivity greatly by reducing to hours, tasks that used to take days to complete manually.

Implementing Strategy

While the first three stages of category management take place at headquarters, the fourth stage—implementing strategies—involves both headquarters personnel and employees at individual stores. During this stage, the category manager and his specialists communicate the specifics of their product mix, pricing, merchandising and promotional tactics to the store where the hands-on responsibilities involved with pricing changes, product stocking, display assembling and positioning, and other tasks are implemented.

This stage is pivotal to category management. The greatest strategic plan and the greatest tactics ever conceived by a category manager will fail if you don't communicate clearly with store managers and employees in your stores about how to implement your plans.

To ensure that all of his planning doesn't go to waste, the category manager must establish a system for routinely relaying the tactical details of merchandising and marketing plans to individual stores. These communications, among other things, should provide merchandising plans, including planograms; advertising plans, including products to feature in circulars; promotion plans, with display placement details; pricing changes, including new shelf labels and cash-register prices; new products, with stocking instructions; and discontinued products, with removal dates.

**The Category Manager
Relays Information:**

Category Manager

- Merchandising plans
- Planograms
- Advertising plans
- Promotion plans
- Price changes
- Shelf labels
- Stocking instructions
- Discontinued products

In establishing this system, the category manager should establish strong relationships with store managers and to talk with them often to get their feedback. Store managers often have valuable information about competitors, out-of-stocks or other areas not illuminated by scanning data or market research, and their input enhances the category manager's ability to monitor market-place changes.

Evaluating Results

Reacting quickly to such changes is central to the fifth stage of category management, evaluating results. During this stage, the category manager measures the results of his merchandising and marketing plans, and compares them with his objectives and with his competitors' performance. For example, has he achieved his sales and profit goals for the category?

After seeing whether he has exceeded or fallen short of his objectives, he must determine why. Are there stores where the strategic plan was not implemented properly? Has a new promotion launched by a competitor hurt his business? Is shelf allocation causing out-of-stocks? Or are prices too high?

After answering such questions, the category manager must adjust his tactics quickly to stay on track toward his objectives, or to capitalize on new opportunities to exceed those objectives.

A variety of computer software programs have been developed to help category managers continually evaluate the effectiveness of their strategic plans and to make midstream adjustments.

They include programs that translate scanning statistics into actionable data, including category and market-share data and price differentials.

Competitive price systems also come in handy at this stage, allowing a category manager to compare his prices with competitors' prices, compare actual data versus estimates, and to make appropriate changes. Other programs measure the effectiveness of specific promotions, quantifying the impact of feature ads, displays and price reductions. These programs maintain a history of past promotions for an item that can be used when planning future promotions. Shelf-space management programs can help the category manager answer questions such as:

- Are my shelf quantities correct?
- Am I missing sales opportunities?
- Am I causing extra labor/stocking costs?

Having answered such questions, the category manager can use a shelf-space management program to fine tune his merchandising tactics.

Technological innovations enable the category manager to concentrate on the things he must do to make his business profitable, including thinking creatively, overseeing the activities of specialists, maintaining his relationships with store managers, keeping a close eye on the competition, and developing long-term relationships with trusted suppliers.

Having answered questions regarding quantities, sales opportunities and labor/ stocking costs, the category manager can use a shelf-space management program to fine tune his merchandising tactics.

Retailers Charting New Course With Manufacturers

In theory, category managers could accomplish the five stages of category management without manufacturer input by using in-house information and technology augmented by research and analysis products purchased from third parties.

In reality, this approach is impractical.

For one thing, it's too expensive. Sharing information and technology resources with manufacturers is much more cost-effective than going it alone.

Retailers Checking Out New Ways to Do Business

Information and Technology

Manufacturer   **Retailer**

Sharing information and technology resources between manufacturers and retailers is much more cost-effective than going it alone.

For another, it's too inefficient. The typical category manager doesn't have time to wade through piles of reports about category and consumer trends. He's consumer-oriented and results-oriented, and he needs to cut through data quickly to get to the bottom line in each of these areas.

Specialists can help, but they're also busy developing the tactics necessary to support or refine his merchandising and marketing plans.

Faced with these realities, the category manager usually turns to manufacturers for assistance. One manufacturer could become his category "captain," a respected resource he relies on to provide a big-picture perspective on both the marketplace and his category.

Although retailers now have access to more marketplace data than ever, manufacturers, by virtue of their size and scope, still can provide news and perspective that category managers either can't gain themselves or don't have time to pursue. Compounding the time challenge is the fact that category managers often are handling a learning curve since many don't remain in the same position for more than a couple of years.

Manufacturers, who see the best and worst in stores across the nation, can help strengthen the category manager's knowledge by passing along information about consumer trends, new-product developments, and pricing/merchandising/marketing trends, both nationally and locally. The category manager also can tap manufacturers' broad-based information technology and market research in developing customized merchandising and promotions and evaluating their impact on individual products and the category as a whole.

Manufacturers today are eager to develop such relationships with category managers. With two-thirds of brand purchase decisions now made in the store, manufacturers recognize that their best chance of influencing shoppers is through the retailer. Instead of viewing retailers primarily as mass-market distribution arms, most manufacturers now are vitally interested in helping the retailer to develop merchandising and marketing programs to push products out the door. Manufacturers today must communicate effectively with their targeted consumers at the store. Retailers, in turn, striving to maximize each category, are vitally interested in obtaining the items that can contribute the most to the category.

Meanwhile, as information, technology, and decision support tools continue to improve, both retailers and manufacturers are beginning to recognize the advantages of working more closely together and sharing resources to interpret the wealth of data now coming their way.

Continuing marketplace changes and information technology advances promise to foster the development of a growing number of long-term, mutually beneficial relationships between retailers and manufacturers. In forming such relationships, the category manager must have a keen eye for recognizing not only manufacturer strengths, but also his own limitations, both informationally and technologically.

Today's category managers might be the entrepreneurial shopkeepers of the 1990s, but that doesn't mean they can't seek outside assistance in getting to know their customers better and tailoring their category to meet customer needs. After all, they can't know everything there is to know about shoppers. They're not personally filling each customer's order or talking over the counter with shoppers like their predecessors once did. They need the input of other marketing experts to fill in the

As information, technology, and decision support tools continue to improve, both retailers and manufacturers are beginning to recognize the advantages of working more closely together.

Retailers Checking Out New Ways to Do Business

• • • • • • • • • • • • • • • • •

blanks that still exist, despite modern information and technology. The willingness to seek such assistance is an important step toward successful category management. For, as successful entrepreneurs long have recognized, one of the best ways to grow is to learn from the knowledge and experience of others.

Category Management in Action — a Case in Point

Category management is more than just an attractive concept. It already has been implemented successfully by a number of leading retailers and manufacturers. The scenario that follows is an example of category management in action. The example involves a supermarket chain, SuperProfit Foods; a manufacturer, Debonair, Inc.; and a category, shampoo.

SuperProfit Foods is a full-service retailer that offers shoppers the convenience of one-stop shopping at its high-end food and drug "combo" stores. The chain features a variety of high-quality products at competitive prices but uses promotional pricing as well.

Debonair, Inc. is a mid-sized company that manufactures hair-care products and cosmetics. Among its products are Bargain Bubbles, a budget shampoo, and Elegance, a premium-priced shampoo. Debonair wants to increase Bargain Bubbles' market share and to maximize Elegance's profitability.

In preparing to implement category management, SuperProfit Foods establishes a strategic goal for the shampoo category—it must generate profits. The chain's shampoo category manager sets the category management process in motion by reviewing the category.

1. Reviewing the Category

The category manager begins his category review by examining the shampoo category as a whole and its performance in specific retail outlets.

Through analyses of third-party data for the most recent 52-week period, the category manager determines that during the past year shampoo category sales across all trade outlets nationwide increased 3 percent from the previous year to $1.21 billion. Unit sales increased 1 percent to 556 million, and the average per-unit price climbed 2 percent to $2.17.

Shampoo dollar sales at supermarkets with sales over $2 million increased 2 percent to $603 million, but supermarkets' share of total dollar sales declined 1.2 percent to 50.5 percent. The category generated 6.1 percent of the $9.9 billion in health and beauty aid (HBA) department sales at supermarkets nationwide, and accounted for 0.2 percent of the $360 billion in total supermarket all commodity volume (ACV).

The category manager discovers that the category includes 1,974 active UPCs at supermarkets nationally and that 15 percent of the UPCs were introduced during the last year (see chart 2.3). Each supermarket stocks an average of 235 UPCs, and the UPC stocking mix generates $1.64 per UPC per store per week. This performance ranks 51st among 164 HBA categories.

2.3 Total U.S. Supermarket Dynamics
Shampoo-aerosol, liquid, lotion, powder

52-weeks	# active UPCs	% new UPCs	# UPCs handled	UPC dollar velocity
Category	1,974	15%	235	$1.64
Brands	1,714	16%	229	$1.65
Private label	241	12%	6	$1.33
Generic	19	–	2	$1.00

Source: Nielsen Marketing Research, Nielsen Highlights,Category Performance Report

Retailers Checking Out New Ways to Do Business

After examining supermarket shampoo sales trends, the category manager turns his attention to the category's performance at competing retail outlets, including drug stores and mass merchandisers. Scanning-data analyses provided by a third party show that mass merchandisers have hurt both supermarkets and drug stores in the shampoo category. Mass merchandisers have increased shampoo dollar sales 8.1 percent during the last year, increasing their share of category sales 1.8 percent to 24.5 percent. Like supermarkets, drug stores increased their shampoo sales but saw their category share decline because of mass merchandisers' advances. Drug stores' share of category sales totaled 25.0 percent, compared with 25.6 percent a year earlier (see charts 2.4A and 2.4B).

2.4A Shampoo Dollar Share

Across trade channels

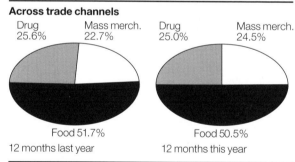

| Drug 25.6% | Mass merch. 22.7% | Drug 25.0% | Mass merch. 24.5% |

Food 51.7%   Food 50.5%

12 months last year   12 months this year

Source: Nielsen Marketing Research, Procision

2.4B Shampoo Growth

Across trade channels

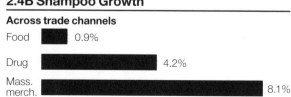

Food   0.9%

Drug   4.2%

Mass. merch.   8.1%

Dollar sales—percent change vs. year-ago

Source: Nielsen Marketing Research, Procision

Having gained a nationwide perspective on the shampoo category, the category manager sets his sights next on SuperProfit Foods' standing within the marketplace. Using scanning-data analyses, he compares the chain's performance on the marketwide, HBA, shampoo-category and shampoo-brand levels against the performance of food stores with annual sales of $4 million or more.

He determines that SuperProfit Foods trailed the market in total dollar sales during the latest 52-week period, experiencing a 4.5 percent decline, compared with a marketwide increase of 1.2 percent. This downward trend carried through the HBA department and the shampoo category at SuperProfit Foods. HBA sales declined 4.3 percent at the chain, compared with a 4.2 percent increase marketwide, while shampoo sales fell 9.7 percent, compared with a virtually flat performance marketwide (see chart 2.5).

2.5 Dollar Sales
Percent Change vs. Year-Ago

	Market		SuperProfit Foods	
	13 weeks	52 weeks	13 weeks	52 weeks
Total dollar sales	+.1	+1.2	-10.6	-4.5
HBA department	+1.5	+4.2	-8.5	-4.3
Shampoo category	-3.5	+.7	-19.6	-9.7

Source: Nielsen Marketing Research, SCAN*FACT PC for Retailers

Retailers Checking Out New Ways to Do Business

• • • • • • • • • • • • • • • •

The category manager calculates SuperProfit Foods' share of total market sales and discovers that neither the chain's HBA category nor its shampoo category is keeping pace with the retailer's overall market share of 18.3 percent (see chart 2.6).

2.6 SuperProfit Foods Market Share

	13 weeks	52 weeks
Total sales	17.2%	18.3%
HBA department	15.1%	15.8%
Shampoo category	15.9%	17.4%

Source: Nielsen Marketing Research , SCAN∗FACT PC for Retailers

To understand the category's contribution to sales, he then analyzes the importance of HBA and shampoo sales to total market sales and to total sales at SuperProfit Foods. He learns that the HBA department and the category account for similar percentages of total sales in each instance, with HBA sales accounting for 5.6 percent of total market sales and 4.8 percent of SuperProfit Foods' sales, and shampoo producing 0.3 percent of total sales marketwide and at the chain.

Knowing that SuperProfit Foods is losing both shampoo sales and market share to its competitors (see chart 2.7), the category manager begins to search for reasons for the losses. How does SuperProfit Foods stack up against the market in terms of product mix, pricing, promotion and distribution? And how do these factors affect the category's performance?

Using a software program that compares item pricing within categories among different types of retail outlets, he finds one of the reasons immediately: Mass merchandisers' shampoo prices are beating

SuperProfit Foods' badly. In fact, all of the 103 key items offered by the chain and mass merchandisers are priced higher at SuperProfit Foods. The chain beats the drug stores' prices on most shampoo items, but it also has a pricing problem with one food-store competitor, labeled Food #2, which matches or beats SuperProfit Foods' prices on all shampoo items (see chart 2.8).

2.7 Shampoo Share and Sales Trends

SuperProfit Foods

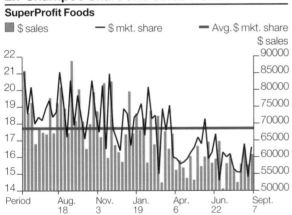

Source: Nielsen Marketing Research, SCAN✱FACT PC for Retailers

2.8 Competitive Price Comparison

Compare: shampoo

	What if	SPFs	Food #1	Mass merch.	Chain drug	Food #2
Sales $:	42,591	42,591	43,666	34,646	44,581	42,271
Contribution:	10,208	10,208	11,283	2,263	12,198	9,888
Gross margin:	23.97	23.97	25.84	6.53	27.36	23.39
B index:		100.00	102.53	81.35	104.67	99.25

Counts of items showing differences from the base zone (SuperProfit Foods)

Competition is higher:	0	87	0	101	0
Competition is same:	103	0	0	0	59
Competition is lower:	0	16	103	2	44
Competition does not carry:	0	0	0	0	0

Source: Nielsen Marketing Research, Nielsen Retail Price Simulator

Chapter 2

Retailers Checking Out New Ways to Do Business

•••••••••••••••••

Seeking more information about how competing food stores manage the shampoo category, the category manager delves deeper into scanning-data analyses to compare the performance of individual shampoo brands at SuperProfit Foods with their performance marketwide. He quickly recognizes a disparity: Bargain Bubbles, a budget shampoo that ranks second in dollar sales market-wide, ranks only fourth at SuperProfit Foods (see chart 2.9). The category manager wants to know why.

2.9 Brand Importance Report for Shampoo
SuperProfit Foods vs. Remaining Market for 13 Weeks

Description	Chain $ sales	Chain rank	Rem. mkt. rank	Rem. mkt. $ sales	Chain mkt. share	Chain cat. impt.	Rem. mkt. cat. impt.
Clean & Soft	108,826	1	1	512,345	17.5	14.5	13.0
1st Impressions	77,672	2	3	370,341	17.3	10.3	9.4
Mane Tame	64,446	3	4	244,160	20.9	8.6	6.2
Bargain Bubbles	56,864	4	2	433,300	11.6	7.6	11.0
Silky Style	43,198	5	6	147,773	22.6	5.8	3.7
Elegance	30,869	6	5	181,075	14.6	4.1	4.6

Source: Nielsen Marketing Research, SCAN∗FACT PC for Retailers

The top three brands at SuperProfit Foods all have much stronger growth rates and much greater market shares than does Bargain Bubbles. A software program that rates brand sales and market-share performance by retailer classifies Bargain Bubbles as a low-growth, low-market share brand at SuperProfit Foods (see chart 2.10).

2.10 Scan❋Diagnosis for Shampoo

Selected brand performance

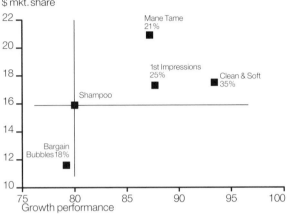

$ mkt. share

Source: Nielsen Marketing Research, SCAN❋FACT PC for Retailers

Looking at specific items within the Bargain Bubbles line, the category manager discovers that the sales leader, a 16-ounce item, ranks only 27th in sales among the 339 shampoo items carried by SuperProfit Foods. The same item ranks 17th in sales among the 878 shampoo items marketwide (see chart 2.11).

2.11 Comparative Rank Report: Shampoo
SuperProfit Foods vs. Remaining Market for 13 Weeks

Item	Chain rank	Rem. mkt. rank	Chain $ sales	Rem. mkt. $ sales	Chain $ mkt. share	Chain cat. $ share	Rem. mkt. cat. $ share
1st Impressions DF N–O Lot.15 oz.	1	2	25,987	77,990	25.0	3.3	1.9
Clean & Soft N Lq.15 oz.	2	1	23,848	96,087	19.9	3.1	2.3
⋮							
Bargain Bubbles X–B Lq.16 oz.	27	17	6,318	30,867	17.0	.8	.7
Silky Style X–B Lq.15 oz.	28	44	6,244	22,041	22.1	.8	.5
1st Impressions DF N–O Lot.11 oz.	29	6	6,226	44,603	12.2	.8	1.1
Glistening X–B Lq.15 oz.	30	28	6,065	27,611	18.0	.8	.7

Source: Nielsen Marketing Research, SCAN❋FACT PC for Retailers

Retailers Checking Out New Ways to Do Business

Bargain Bubbles is clearly underperforming the market at SuperProfit Foods. Suspecting that the cause might be related to promotional activity, the category manager compares promotion frequency for Bargain Bubbles across the market and at SuperProfit Foods. He learns that competitors promote Bargain Bubbles at least twice as often as does SuperProfit Foods during the course of a year (see chart 2.12).

2.12 Promotional Dollar Sales Trends
Bargain Bubbles Shampoo

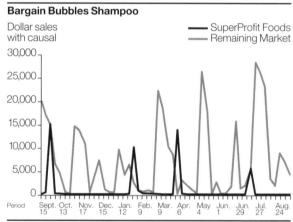

Source: Nielsen Marketing Research, SCAN✱FACT PC for Retailers

Knowing the key role that pricing plays in many purchase decisions, the category manager also compares SuperProfit Foods' pricing strategy for Bargain Bubbles with that of the market. He discovers that the chain's everyday non-promotional price for Bargain Bubbles is 17 cents to 32 cents higher than it is elsewhere (see chart 2.13).

2.13 Everyday Non-Promotional Pricing Report For Bargain Bubbles Shampoo Items SuperProfit Foods vs. Remaining Market for 13 Weeks

Item	Chain ev./day price	Rem. mkt. ev./day price	Price differ.
Bargain Bubbles X-B Lq. 12 oz.	$1.39	$1.07	.32
Bargain Bubbles O Lq. 16 oz.	$1.46	$1.17	.29
Bargain Bubbles SF Lq. 16 oz.	$1.50	$1.22	.28
Bargain Bubbles DF N-O Lot. 16 oz.	$1.46	$1.18	.28
Bargain Bubbles ND Lq. 12 oz.	$1.39	$1.12	.27
Bargain Bubbles STR Lq. 16 oz.	$1.47	$1.19	.28
Bargain Bubbles MS X-B Lq. 16 oz.	$1.46	$1.20	.26
Bargain Bubbles MS Lq. 16 oz.	$1.42	$1.17	.25

Source: Nielsen Marketing Research, SCAN*FACT PC for Retailers

During Bargain Bubbles' promotions, SuperProfit Foods offers larger-percentage price discounts than do competitors so it can come close to matching their promotional prices. But because competitors run more promotions, the impact of SuperProfit Foods' promotional pricing strategy is limited (see chart 2.14).

2.14 Promotion Report: For Bargain Bubbles Shampoo Items Remaining Market for 13 Weeks

Item	Sales dollars	% sales on promo.	Avg. non-promo. price	Avg. promo. price	% of discount
Bargain Bubbles STR Lq. 16 oz.	39,155	37.9	$1.19	$.96	19.3%
Bargain Bubbles ND Lq. 16 oz.	37,054	36.2	$1.21	$.95	21.6%
Bargain Bubbles H R Lq. 16 oz.	31,325	30.0	$1.24	$.94	24.4%
Bargain Bubbles X-B Lq. 16 oz.	30,867	29.6	$1.25	$.94	24.9%
Bargain Bubbles MS X-B Lq. 16 oz.	28,512	36.6	$1.20	$.95	20.5%
Bargain Bubbles X-B Lq. 12 oz.	23,940	19.9	$1.07	$1.01	5.7%

SuperProfit Foods for 13 Weeks

Item	Sales dollars	% sales on promo.	Avg. non-promo. price	Avg. promo. price	% of discount
Bargain Bubbles X-B Lq. 16 oz.	6,318	12.4	$1.46	$.99	32.3%
Bargain Bubbles H R Lq. 16 oz.	5,759	10.0	$1.47	$.99	32.5%
Bargain Bubbles ND Lq. 16 oz.	5,382	11.4	$1.46	$.99	32.1%
Bargain Bubbles STR Lq. 16 oz.	5,163	11.0	$1.47	$.99	32.5%
Bargain Bubbles O Lq. 16 oz.	4,687	11.8	$1.46	$.99	32.3%
Bargain Bubbles N Lq. 16 oz.	4,172	12.6	$1.46	$.99	32.2%

Source: Nielsen Marketing Research, SCAN*FACT PC for Retailers

Retailers Checking Out New Ways to Do Business

• • • • • • • • • • • • • • • •

The category manager next compares the Bargain Bubbles product mix at SuperProfit Foods with the brands' marketwide product mix. Although the chain and the market carry similar Bargain Bubbles item sizes, the market far outdistances SuperProfit Foods in terms of both the number and type of Bargain Bubbles items offered (see chart 2.15).

2.15 Product Mix Summary Report
Shampoo Dollar Sales–13 Weeks

	Clean & Soft	1st Impressions	Mane Tame	Bargain Bubbles	Silky Style	Elegance	Private Label
Items carried							
SPF	25	25	15	21	13	5	7
Rem. mkt.	25	39	28	42	20	16	28
Sizes carried							
SPF	6	6	6	2	4	1	4
Rem. mkt.	7	10	11	3	5	4	6
Types carried							
SPF	6	7	6	19	4	5	6
Rem. mkt.	6	10	8	32	5	7	21

Source: Nielsen Marketing Research, SCAN✳FACT PC for Retailers

This information, coupled with Bargain Bubbles' comparatively poor sales performance at SuperProfit Foods, leads the category manager to examine his product mix and ensure that he is providing the Bargain Bubbles items and types that are in demand in the chain's trading areas.

Using software applications, he generates two reports: The first lists the Bargain Bubbles items not offered by SuperProfit Foods and the sales they generate elsewhere in the market (see chart 2.16); the second lists slow-moving items across the shampoo category at SuperProfit Foods (see chart 2.17).

By comparing the two reports, the category manager can determine whether certain products should be delisted to make room for Bargain Bubbles items with greater sales potential. Before making delisting and authorization decisions for individual SuperProfit Foods stores, however, he must know more about the types of consumers in SuperProfit Foods' trading areas, their purchase behavior and their needs.

2.16 Items Not Handled/Sales Potential Report for Bargain Bubbles Shampoo Items With Sales in the Remaining Market But Not Handled by SuperProfit Foods for 13 Weeks

Item	Rem. mkt. $ sales	Sub-category impt.	Avg. % stores selling	% sales with causal	Avg. selling price	Est. chain sales
Bargain Bubbles VIT REG Lq. 16 oz.	12,038	.3	23%	31.8	$1.09	8,343
Bargain Bubbles RS REG Lq. 16 oz.	6,923	.2	26%	14.2	$1.26	4,197
Bargain Bubbles Lemon Lq. 16 oz.	4,291	.1	17%	13.8	$1.23	4,037
Bargain Bubbles T Lq. 16 oz.	3,654	.1	16%	49.7	$1.02	3,550
Bargain Bubbles GLD Lq. 16 oz.	3,194	.1	17%	2.6	$1.25	2,965
Bargain Bubbles DF ND Lot. 16 oz.	1,953	.0	14%	14.3	$1.18	2,282

Source: Nielsen Marketing Research, SCAN✳FACT PC for Retailers

2.17 Slow Mover Report: Shampoo For SuperProfit Foods—13 Weeks vs. Year-Ago

Item	Chain $ sales	Chain mkt. share	Chain sub-cat. impt.	Rem. mkt. growth	Chain growth	Chain avg. % stores selling
Golden JJB Lq. T3 oz.	3	9.9	.0	-51.2	-50.0	0%
1st Impressions DF ND Lot. 11 oz.	10	.7	.0	-59.4	-99.4	0%
Gentle GLD Lq. 11 oz.	11	100.0	.0	-100.0	9.6	0%
Golden AV Lq. T3 oz.	12	22.4	.0	13.2	-69.2	1%
Suds PB Lq. 8 oz.	14	.6	.0	107.1	2.9	0%
Silky Style X-B Lq. 18 oz.	14	1.6	.0	-65.6	-99.5	0%

Source: Nielsen Marketing Research, SCAN✳FACT PC for Retailers

Retailers Checking Out New Ways to Do Business

2. Targeting Consumers

SuperProfit Foods uses a demographic and purchase-behavior database to identify "clusters" of consumers living in its trading areas. Clusters are groups of households with similar lifestyles, as determined by factors such as income, education level, occupation, number of children and home ownership. The chain utilizes a 47-cluster system that identifies clusters ranging from mature professionals with large families that include teenagers, to young, low-income single people living in apartments. Certain clusters appear to be predominant in the chains' trading areas (see chart 2.18).

2.18 SuperProfit Foods Trade Areas

Shampoo—Aerosol, Liquid, Lotion
Base: Households

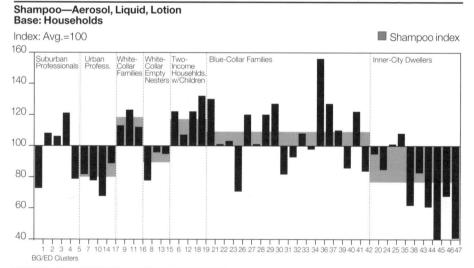

Source: Nielsen Marketing Research, ClusterPLUS, Nielsen Household Services

Consumer analyses show that demographic characteristics such as income strongly influence shampoo purchases. Using consumer analyses, the category manager identifies three groups of household clusters—Upscale Affluent, Middle Income Families, and Inner City—which have distinct differences in their demographics and shampoo purchasing (see chart 2.19).

2.19 SuperProfit Foods
Three Target Groups For Shampoo Planograms

Target group	Types of households	Distribution of households within SuperProfit Foods trade areas	Distribution of households shopping in SuperProfit Foods stores	Shampoo index
1	Upscale Affluent - Suburban Professionals - Urban Professionals - White-Collar Empy Nesters	38.7	43.5	90
2	Middle Income Families - White-Collar Families - Two-Income Households with Children - Blue-Collar Families	39.5	34.7	118
3	Inner City - Inner City Dwellers	21.9	21.8	71

Source: Nielsen Marketing Research, ClusterPLUS, Nielsen Household Services

The category manager recognizes that maximizing the category's potential requires merchandising shampoo differently for each household cluster group. Since he knows which cluster groups reside within the trading area of each store, the category manager segments SuperProfit Foods stores into three types for the shampoo category—Upscale Affluent, Middle Income Families, and Inner City—based on the concentration of each cluster group in the store's trading area. He then develops a customized merchandising strategy for each store type, including product mix, pricing, promotion, shelf space and inventory, based on the shampoo buying behavior of consumers in the store's trading area. To do so, he takes a closer look at the characteristics of the three target groups.

Retailers Checking Out New Ways to Do Business

• • • • • • • • • • • • • • • • • Target Group 1, labeled Upscale Affluent, includes Suburban and Urban Professionals, as well as White-Collar Empty Nesters. A typical consumer in this group might drive an imported luxury car, downhill ski, employ a maid, play tennis, golf or racquetball, and travel abroad. These consumers also display a propensity toward buying table wines, bottled water, whole coffee beans, and imported beer (see chart 2.20).

Although Upscale Affluent consumers typically buy premium-priced brands, purchase behavior data tells him they are not the heaviest buyers of shampoo. He also learns that SuperProfit Foods already is attracting a higher-than-expected percentage of these consumers (see chart 2.19). Now the category manager can develop a shampoo assortment featuring upscale brands and premium prices for the Upscale Affluent stores of SuperProfit Foods.

2.20 Lifestyles of Target Group 1
Upscale Affluent

Index

176	Own Any Imported Luxury Car
163	Bennigan's
161	Own Downhill Ski Boots
161	Housekeeping Services Used in Past Year: Maid
161	Sports Attend: Tennis
157	Foreign Travel: Have Passport
155	Own Downhill Skis
153	Fuddrucker's
152	Foreign Travel Past 3 Years: Vacation
147	Sports Attend: Golf
146	Foreign Travel Past 3 Years: Any
145	Participated Past Year: Attend Live Theatre
143	All Users: Imported Dinner/Table Wines
143	Own Raquetball Raquet
143	All Users: Domestic Dinner/Table Wines
141	Sports Attend: Ice Hockey
139	Participated Past Year: Attend Music/Dance Perfs.
139	All Users : Bottled Water
138	HH Property Maint. Past Year: Lawn Maint. Service
138	Own Raquetball Balls
136	Participated Past Year: Concerts On Radio
135	Expense Last 6 Mos.: Dry Cleaning
135	Own Golf Clubs
135	Participated Past Year: Health Club/Gym Workout
134	Friendly's
135	Own Golf Balls
133	All Users: Whole Coffee Beans
133	Own Cross-Country Ski Boots
132	Casino Gambling/Past Year
132	Own Cross-Country Skis
132	Sports Attend: Football-Weekend Prof'l Games
131	All Users: Imported Beer
131	Sports Listen on Radio: Ice Hockey

Source: Nielsen Marketing Research, ClusterPLUS, Nielsen Household Services, MRI

Chapter 2

Retailers Checking Out New Ways to Do Business

• • • • • • • • • • • • • • • • •

Target Group 2, labeled Middle Income Families, includes White-Collar Families, Blue-Collar Families and Two-Income Households with Children. A typical consumer in this group might own a camper/trailer, purchase lawn care products, bowl, play racquetball and downhill ski. These consumers also like to participate in aerobic exercise, play video games and attend sports events (see chart 2.21).

Consumer analyses show that Middle Income Families are heavy buyers of shampoo and typically purchase budget brands. However, SuperProfit Foods is not attracting its fair share of these households (see chart 2.19). The chain has an opportunity to boost its shampoo sales and market share by customizing its shampoo merchandising to attract more Middle Income Families. It also supports the idea of delisting certain slow-moving brands in favor of adding certain Bargain Bubbles items. Based on these findings, the category manager develops a customized shampoo strategy for SuperProfit Foods' Middle Income Families stores. Under the strategy, the category's product mix, shelf space, inventory and merchandising all are tilted toward budget brands.

The category manager also does his own market-basket analysis to identify other products that—when promoted—are likely to attract Middle Income Families. The products, which can be promoted concurrently with Bargain Bubbles, include vitamins, mouthwash, cosmetics and pain relievers from the HBA department as well as products from other departments.

2.21 Lifestyles of Target Group 2
Middle Income Families

Index

171	HH Prop. Maint. Past Yr.: Pool Chemicals
159	HH Owns Towable Folding Tent Camper
155	HH Owns Truck Mounted Camper
146	HH Prop. Maint. Past Yr.: Lawn Insecticides
145	Own Raquetball Balls
144	HH Owns Other Camper/Trailer
143	HH Prop. Maint. Past Yr.: Lawn Fert. W/Weed Control
141	Own Raquetball Raquet
140	HH Furn. Bought Past Yr.: Upholstery Fabric
140	HH Prop. Maint. Past Yr.: Lawn Fert. W/O Weed Control
137	HH Prop. Maint. Past Yr.: Weed Killer
135	HH Prop. Maint. Past Yr.: Lawn Maint. Service
133	Sizzler Family Steak Houses
131	Participated Past Yr.: Model-Making
130	Sports Attend: Soccer
129	Own Bowling Balls
129	Own Sportswatch/Chronogr.
129	HH Furn. Bought Past Yr.: Wall To Wall Carpet
128	Own Tennis Balls
128	Fuddrucker's
127	HH Prop. Maint. Past Yr.: Trees
127	Participated Past Yr.: Video Games
127	Own Golf Balls
127	Arby's
126	HH Prop. Maint. Past Yr.: Lawn Seed
125	HH Prop. Maint. Past Yr.: Shrubs/Plants-Outdoor
124	Own Golf Clubs
124	Own Tennis Raquet
124	HH Prop. Maint. Past Yr.: Garden Insecticide
124	Participated Past Yr.: Aerobic Exercise
123	Bennigan's
122	Sports Attend: Football-Weekend Prof'l Games
122	Participated Past Yr.: Backgammon
122	Engage in: Tropical Fish
122	Own Downhill Skis
122	Sports Attend: Basketball-Prof'l

Source: Nielsen Marketing Research, ClusterPLUS, Nielsen Household Services, MRI

Retailers Checking Out New Ways to Do Business

• • • • • • • • • • • • • • • • Target Group 3, labeled Inner City, consists of Inner City Dwellers who frequently attend sports events, watch them on TV, or listen to them on the radio. Many also use a laundry, go to the movies, purchase alcoholic beverages, visit fast-food restaurants, consume soft drinks, and use instant or freeze-dried coffee (see chart 2.22).

2.22 Lifestyles of Target Group 3
Inner City

Index	
150	Expense Last 6 Mos.: Laundries and Laundromats
147	Sports Listen on Radio: Boxing
127	Sports Attend: Boxing
124	Sports Attend: Football-Monday Night Prof'l Games
118	All Users: Rum
117	All Users: Imported Beer
116	All Users: Port, Sherry & Dessert Wines
116	Attended 4+ Movies/Past 3 Months
114	Sports Watch on TV: Soccer
112	Sports Attend: Basketball-Prof'l
112	Sports Attend: Soccer
112	All Users: Super Premium Domestic Beer
110	Popeye's Famous Fried Chicken
108	Sports Listen on Radio: Basketball-Prof'l
108	All Users: Premium Domestic Beer
108	All Users: Rye or Blended Whiskey
107	All Users: Sangria, Party, Pop Wines
107	All Users: Popular Domestic Beer
107	Sports Watch on TV: Wrestling-Prof'l
107	Kentucky Fried Chicken
106	All Users: Canadian Whiskey
105	Sports Watch on TV: Weight Lifting
105	All Users: Regular Domestic Beer
104	All Users: Regular Cola Drinks, Not Diet
103	Foreign Travel Past 3 Yrs.: Vacation
101	Sports Watch on TV: Track & Field
101	Sports Listen on Radio: Football-Mon. Night
100	Casino Gambling/Past Year

Source: Nielsen Marketing Research, ClusterPLUS, Nielsen Household Services, MRI

By analyzing purchase-behavior data, the category manager determines that Inner City consumers are about 30 percent less likely to buy shampoo than is the average consumer. He also learns that SuperProfit Foods attracts its fair share of Inner City consumers (see chart 2.19). He concludes that this group is not a prime target for increasing shampoo sales and develops his merchandising strategy for Inner City stores accordingly. The category manager develops a shampoo assortment featuring brands and prices for the Inner City stores of SuperProfit Foods.

In addition to his own analysis, the category manager obtains consumer information from Debonair, Inc., the manufacturer of Bargain Bubbles shampoo. The team sales leader, or sales representative, for Debonair has prepared a presentation for Super-Profit Foods during which he shares findings he has obtained through his own research and analyses.

He shows how lower prices are causing shampoo buyers to shift their outlet preference for the shampoo category away from food stores (see pages 133-143 in **Targeting Consumers** section of **Chapter 3** for this detailed analysis). He further shows that Middle Income Families appear to offer the best growth potential for the shampoo category at SuperProfit Foods and demonstrates the important role Bargain Bubbles plays in "re-attracting" Middle Income Families who are switching

• • • • • • • • • • • • • •

their shampoo purchases to non-food outlets (see pages 133-143 in **Targeting Consumers** section of **Chapter 3** for this detailed analysis). He proposes a strategy for helping SuperProfit Foods attract its fair share of Middle Income Families and demonstrates the category impact of merchandising and promoting the Bargain Bubbles brand (see pages 144-151 in **Planning Merchandising** section of **Chapter 3** for this detailed analysis).

In addition, the team sales leader explains that Debonair is launching Bargain Bubbles advertising targeted at Middle Income Families. The advertising, he adds, will produce indirect benefits for SuperProfit Foods' Middle Income Families stores, especially if the chain features Bargain Bubbles prominently in these locations (see pages 133-143 in **Targeting Consumers** section of **Chapter 3** for this detailed analysis).

The presentation by the Bargain Bubbles team sales leader, which includes a discussion of allowances provided by Debonair or required by SuperProfit Foods, helps to round out the category manager's thinking about how to target Middle Income Families. The meeting is part of an ongoing relationship between the manufacturer and the retailer.

3. Planning Merchandising

By this point, it's clear to the category manager that to improve the category's performance, he must customize his merchandising based on the types of consumers that shop at specific stores. He also recognizes that Middle Income Families offer the greatest growth potential for the category, and that Bargain Bubbles is a brand with appeal among Middle Income Families that can increase store traffic and improve the category's performance. These thoughts are uppermost in his mind as he develops a merchandising plan for the category, beginning with determining the best product mix for certain stores and continuing with the development of strategies for pricing, promotion and shelf space.

To determine the optimum product mix for the category in SuperProfit Foods' three types of stores, he compares data on slow-moving items with data showing the sales performance of items not offered by SuperProfit Foods. He then identifies new items that would appeal to each of the chain's three target consumer groups. For example, he looks for strong performers among upscale, premium-priced brands, such as Elegance items, that might be added to the shampoo assortment for SuperProfit Foods' Upscale Affluent stores. He is particularly mindful of budget shampoos, such as Bargain Bubbles, that would enhance the appeal of SuperProfit Foods in the eyes of Middle Income Families.

Based on these analyses, he develops a delisting and authorization plan. It includes the addition of another 16-ounce Bargain Bubbles item and several other brands at Middle Income Families stores, and the delisting of a 12-ounce Bargain Bubbles size and several other brands at those same stores.

Retailers Checking Out New Ways to Do Business

After determining the product assortment, the category manager decides that SuperProfit Foods should implement an everyday lower pricing strategy to help its Middle Income Families stores attract new shoppers—particularly the many who now buy shampoo at mass merchandisers—and to achieve the sales and profit objectives established by the chain for the shampoo category.

He wants to offer prices that are more competitive with mass merchandisers' prices on all key items, but especially on Bargain Bubbles items and Clean & Soft items which currently account for 38 percent of the sales generated by the 103 key shampoo items at SuperProfit Foods. By doing this, he believes, SuperProfit Foods automatically will become more competitive with drug stores and other food stores, too.

The category manager uses a software program to model the impact of various pricing scenarios on category and brand performance at SuperProfit Foods and its competitors. The program allows him to combine information about competitors' prices on the 103 key items with internal scanning or warehouse movement data to develop a variety of "what if" scenarios. These models enable the category manager to measure the impact that raising or lowering prices might have on category sales and gross margins, and on competitive pricing.

To conduct his analysis, the category manager combines SuperProfit Foods' internal data with pricing information from two food-store competitors, a mass merchandiser and a chain drug store (see chart 2.23). Because the category manager is interested primarily in making SuperProfit Foods more competitive with mass merchandisers, this example focuses on price comparisons between SuperProfit Foods and the mass merchandiser.

The category manager sees that the mass merchandiser offers lower prices than SuperProfit Foods on all 103 key items, and has a gross margin of 6.53 for those items compared with SuperProfit Foods' 23.97 (see chart 2.23). He immediately decides that he will try to price those items more competitively with the mass merchandiser to attract more customers, but will not try to match the mass merchandiser's gross margin, because the mass merchandiser's cost advantages are too great.

2.23 Competitive Price Comparison

Compare: shampoo

	What if	SPFs	Food #1	Mass merch.	Chain drug	Food #2
Sales $:	42,591	42,591	43,666	34,646	44,581	42,271
Contribution:	10,208	10,208	11,283	2,263	12,198	9,888
Gross margin:	23.97	23.97	25.84	6.53	27.36	23.39
B index:		100.00	102.53	81.35	104.67	99.25

Counts of items showing differences from the base zone (SuperProfit Foods)

Competition is higher:	0	87	0	101	0
Competition is same:	103	0	0	0	59
Competition is lower:	0	16	103	2	44
Competition does not carry:	0	0	0	0	0

Source: Nielsen Marketing Research, Nielsen Retail Price Simulator

Retailers Checking Out New Ways to Do Business

•••••••••••••••• Using the price-modeling program, he first examines current pricing for Bargain Bubbles, Clean & Soft and other brands at SuperProfit Foods and competitors, as well as the impact of pricing on category and brand sales and gross margins at SuperProfit Foods (see charts 2.24 and 2.25). Charts 2.24 and 2.25 typify the pricing disparity he finds between SuperProfit Foods and the mass merchandiser: For a group of 11 selected products, the mass merchandiser beats SuperProfits Foods' prices by anywhere from 30 cents to 82 cents. The price differential on the three 16-ounce Bargain Bubbles items in the group is 31 cents, and the differential on the three 15-ounce Clean & Soft items is 82 cents.

2.24 Item Price Simulation

	Original	Current		
			Simulation target:	23.97
Sales $:	42,591	42,591	Current gross margin:	23.97
Contribution:	10,208	10,208	Needed change gross:	23.97
Gross margin:	23.97	23.97	Needed change retail:	0.00

UPC description	Movement	Cost	Price what if	G.M. % what if
Clean & Soft Shampoo & C. N 15 oz.	1,498	2.980	3.89	23.39
Clean & Soft Shampoo & C D 15 oz.	661	2.980	3.89	23.39
Clean & Soft Shampoo & C. O 15 oz.	615	2.980	3.89	23.39
1st Impressions Shampoo ND 15 oz.	482	3.590	3.99	10.03
Clean & Soft Shampoo & C. X-B 15 oz.	303	2.980	3.89	23.39
Bargain Bubbles Shampoo HN 16 oz.	303	0.950	1.49	36.24
Bargain Bubbles Shampoo LM 16 oz.	265	0.950	1.49	36.24
Bargain Bubbles Shampoo FRS 16 oz.	257	0.950	1.49	36.24
1st Impressions Shampoo O 15 oz.	253	3.590	3.99	10.03
Clean & Soft Shampoo & C. GTL 22 oz.	249	4.290	5.39	20.41
Elegance Shampoo X-B 15 oz.	249	1.830	2.43	24.69

Source: Nielsen Marketing Research, Nielsen Retail Price Simulator

2.25 Item Price Comparison

	Original	Current		
Sales $:	42,591	42,591	Simulation target:	23.97
Contribution:	10,208	10,208	Current gross margin:	23.97
Gross margin:	23.97	23.97	Needed change gross:	23.97
			Needed change retail:	0.00

UPC description	Price what if	Price SPFs	Price food #1	Price mass merch.	Price chain drug	Price food #2
Clean & Soft Shampoo & C. N 15 oz.	3.89	3.89	4.00	3.07	4.08	3.85
Clean & Soft Shampoo & C. D 15 oz.	3.89	3.89	4.00	3.07	4.08	3.85
Clean & Soft Shampoo & C. O 15 oz.	3.89	3.89	4.00	3.07	4.08	3.85
1st Impressions Shampoo ND 15 oz.	3.99	3.99	4.11	3.69	4.06	3.99
Clean & Soft Shampoo & C. X-B 15 oz.	3.89	3.89	4.00	3.07	4.08	3.85
Bargain Bubbles Shampoo HN 16 oz.	1.49	1.49	1.45	1.18	1.53	1.45
Bargain Bubbles Shampoo LM 16 oz.	1.49	1.49	1.45	1.18	1.53	1.45
Bargain Bubbles Shampoo FRS 16 oz.	1.49	1.49	1.45	1.18	1.53	1.45
1st. Impressions Shampoo O 15 oz.	3.99	3.99	4.11	3.69	4.06	3.99
Clean & Soft Shampoo & C. GTL 22 oz.	5.39	5.39	5.55	4.59	5.61	5.33
Elegance Shampoo X-B 15 oz.	2.43	2.43	2.50	1.92	2.56	2.43

Source: Nielsen Marketing Research, Nielsen Retail Price Simulator

The category manager models a variety of different prices for Bargain Bubbles and Clean & Soft to determine their impact on category and brand sales and gross margins. He evaluates price spreads between private-label and national brands, sets parity pricing on different sizes of the same items, and develops equality groups to make sure that items of the same size and costs are priced in the same manner.

He finally decides on a pricing strategy that brings SuperProfit Foods' prices—particularly those of Bargain Bubbles and Clean & Soft items—much closer to those of the mass merchandiser. Under the strategy, for example, the mass merchandiser's price-differential advantage over SuperProfit Foods on the 11 selected products now ranges from 11 cents to 78 cents, with only an 11-cent edge versus 31 cents on the three 16-ounce Bargain Bubbles

Retailers Checking Out New Ways to Do Business

· · · · · · · · · · · · · · · · ·   items in the group, and only a 42-cent advantage versus 82 cents on the three 15-ounce Clean & Soft items (see chart 2.26).

2.26 Item Price Comparison

	Original	Current		
			Simulation target:	20.82
Sales $:	42,591	40,904	Current gross margin:	20.83
Contribution:	10,208	8,521	Needed change gross:	22.75
Gross margin:	23.97	20.83	Needed change retail:	-0.02

UPC description	Price what if	Price SPFs	Price food #1	Price mass merch.	Price chain drug	Price food #2
Clean & Soft Shampoo & C. N 15 oz.	3.49	3.89	4.00	3.07	4.08	3.85
Clean & Soft Shampoo & C. D 15 oz.	3.49	3.89	4.00	3.07	4.08	3.85
Clean & Soft Shampoo & C. O 15 oz.	3.49	3.89	4.00	3.07	4.08	3.85
1st Impressions Shampoo ND 15 oz.	3.98	3.99	4.11	3.69	4.06	3.99
Clean & Soft Shampoo & C. X-B 15 oz.	3.49	3.89	4.00	3.07	4.08	3.85
Bargain Bubbles Shampoo HN 16 oz.	1.29	1.49	1.45	1.18	1.53	1.45
Bargain Bubbles Shampoo LM 16 oz.	1.29	1.49	1.45	1.18	1.53	1.45
Bargain Bubbles Shampoo FRS 16 oz.	1.29	1.49	1.45	1.18	1.53	1.45
1st Impressions Shampoo O 15 oz.	3.98	3.99	4.11	3.69	4.06	3.99
Clean & Soft Shampoo & C. GTL 22 oz.	5.37	5.39	5.55	4.59	5.61	5.33
Elegance Shampoo X-B 15 oz.	2.42	2.43	2.50	1.92	2.56	2.43

Source: Nielsen Marketing Research, Nielsen Retail Price Simulator

2.27 Competitive Price Comparison

Compare: shampoo

	What if	SPFs	Food #1	Mass merch.	Chain drug	Food #2
Sales $:	40,904	42,591	43,666	34,646	44,581	42,271
Contribution:	8,521	10,208	11,283	2,263	12,198	9,888
Gross margin:	20.83	23.97	25.84	6.53	27.36	23.39
B index:		104.03	106.75	84.70	108.99	103.34

Counts of items showing differences from the base zone (SuperProfit Foods)

Competition is higher:	96	103	0	101	78
Competition is same:	6	0	0	0	2
Competition is lower:	1	0	103	2	23
Competition does not carry:	0	0	0	0	0

Source: Nielsen Marketing Research, Nielsen Retail Price Simulator

The new pricing strategy makes SuperProfit Foods more competitive not only with the mass merchandiser's prices for Bargain Bubbles and Clean & Soft, but also with the prices of the chain drug store and the two other food stores (see chart 2.27). SuperProfit Foods now will beat the prices of the first food store for all 103 key items, and will beat the second food store's prices on 78 items. It will also have lower prices than the chain drug store on 101 of the items.

By lowering its prices, SuperProfit Foods will see its gross margin shrink 3.14 percent to 20.83 percent. However, the new pricing strategy, coupled with feature advertising and cross-promotional activity, should enable SuperProfit Foods to capitalize on the importance of the shampoo category to Middle Income Families and to lure more of these shoppers away from competitors' outlets and into its stores. These additional shoppers and their added purchases in other departments should offset the gross-margin reduction in the shampoo category, thus increasing overall profit.

After devising an everyday pricing strategy for the category, the category manager turns his attention to promotions. His key objective in this area is to increase traffic in Middle Income Families stores through aggressive promotion of Bargain Bubbles items and the development of cross-promotions involving other HBA items. Important considerations include the gross margin dictated by the category manager's budget and promotional allowances provided by manufacturers.

Based on Debonair's presentation, he knows he can promote the Bargain Bubbles line of 16-ounce items at a sale price of $1.09, a 40-cent savings over the regular price at Middle Income Families stores. This probably would promote brand switching among

Retailers Checking Out New Ways to Do Business

shoppers at SuperProfit Foods. It also probably would lure shoppers from local mass merchandisers, whose everyday Bargain Bubbles price would be 9 cents higher than SuperProfit Foods' sales price. The category manager also knows that other manufacturers' deals will allow cross-promotion of Bargain Bubbles with three other HBA items.

Using a promotion-planning software program, he can make all merchandising and quantity decisions for an entire "family" of promoted products—in this case, the 16-ounce Bargain Bubbles items—by entering information for a "master" item. He can use the program to confirm regular, non-promotion cost, price, gross margin and forecasted movement for the items. He can also confirm deal information, including the unit deal cost of 0.85 cents. He then enters available co-operative lump-sum allowances and information about proposed merchandising treatments, including the $1.09 sale price (22.02 percent gross margin expected from the promotion), a quarter-page feature ad, and an aisle display with an 8-inch by 12-inch sign. Finally, he enters a quantity estimate based on third-party models or historical data from similar promotions (see chart 2.28).

2.28 Item Promotion Detail

Program B mailer-groc.
Item 00-01000 H Bargain Bubbles

Master Item
Size 16 oz. Pack 6

Regular
Cost 0.950   Price 1.49   GM% 36.24

Forecast (case)
Family 395   Item 36

Deal		Co–op		Quantities	
Unit OI	0.100	Family promo.	1000	Family qty. est. (case)	2,400
Unit B.B.	0.000	Family COG	1000	Item qty. est. (case)	217
Unit cost	0.850	GM% w/co–op	28.3	Model qty. est. (case)	2,268
				Model sales multiplier	5.750

Merchandising

Coupon   Amt.0.00
Sale price   1.09
SL GM%   22.02

Ad   Qtr.   Display ENDL   Sign 8x12

Source: Nielsen Marketing Research, Nielsen Promotion Management System

The category manager projects the sales and gross-margin impact of his promotion strategy—by category and department—by entering into the software program information about all the products that will be promoted, including the Bargain Bubbles items and three other HBA items. He determines that the promotion will produce a gross margin of 28.70 percent, which exceeds his budgeted gross-margin objective of 28 percent. Knowing this, he can elect to "heat up" the sale prices or to "bank" the extra gross-margin dollars. If he chooses to change prices, he can easily measure the impact.

Ultimately, the weekly promotion data from each category manager can be consolidated by department to estimate the impact of all promotions on total chain sales and gross margins (see chart 2.29). This enables management to identify key sources of promotional sales and gross margins, and to compare sales and gross-margin estimates against the chain's sales and gross-margin objectives. In this case, the gross-margin estimate for the chain from a week's worth of promotions totals 24.14 percent. If the chain's weekly gross-margin objective for promotions is greater than 24.14 percent, further changes would be required in one or more promotions to achieve the chain's goal.

2.29 Total Sales Projection
Summarize: Area by Division—Program Week

Division	Cases	Sales $	% Prm. SL	GM $	% Prm. GM	GM %
Division GM	12,250	419,334	7.34	116,192	13.55	27.71
Division GR	190,787	3,981,638	69.69	440,254	51.37	11.06
Division PE	31,500	1,311,930	22.96	300,462	35.06	22.90
Promotion:	Sales $ 5,712,901		% Tot. sls. 28.66	GM $ 856,907		GM % 15.00
Regular:	Sales $ 14,217,099		% Tot. sls. 71.33	GM $ 3,953,775		GM % 27.81
Total:	Sales $ 19,930,001		% Tot. sls. 100.00	GM $ 4,810,682		GM % 24.14

Source: Nielsen Marketing Research, Nielsen Promotion Management System

• • • • • • • • • • • • • • • •

After promotions are locked in, the category manager produces reports to communicate promotion details to store and headquarters management, to monitor co-op allowances, to compare promotion results to promotion estimates, and to maintain a promotion database where the details and results of promotions can be stored for future reference.

Having established a promotional strategy, the category manager begins to examine the issue of shelf space. Besides increasing the sales and profitability of the shampoo category, SuperProfit Foods wants to increase inventory turns and keep inventory costs under control, while eliminating out-of-stocks. The challenge for the category manager is to have the right product, in the right store, in the right quantity. He is particularly interested in allotting appropriate shelf space to Bargain Bubbles in SuperProfit Foods' Middle Income Families stores.

To meet these challenges, he uses a shelf-space management software program to produce store-specific planograms for SuperProfit Foods' Upscale Affluent, Middle Income Families and Inner City stores. Each planogram is more than just a picture of products on shelves; it is the ultimate expression of the entire merchandising process.

In generating the planograms, the program integrates demographic data, purchase-behavior data, scanning data and fixture measurements for each store. The program also takes into account the strategic objectives for the category in the following areas: customer service, out-of-stocks, labor and handling costs, minimum shelf requirements, sales, profits, and return on inventory investment. Fed this data, the program automatically can produce store-specific planograms that reflect each store's unique potential but stay within the company's strategic goals and objectives.

In developing a planogram for SuperProfit Foods' Middle Income Families stores, the category manager first determines the merchandising, marketing and financial objectives for the shampoo category in those stores. In terms of merchandising, he doesn't want any shelf higher than 68 inches; he also wants no backroom stock sales for non-promotional items and a minimum of 1-1/2 cases in shelf holding power. His chief marketing goal is a customer service level of 99 percent, and his top financial goals include less than a 10-day supply, 24 turns annually for the category, base (non-promotional) weekly sales of $40,000 and base weekly profits of $10,000.

The category manager's merchandising objectives reflect SuperProfit Foods' overall merchandising philosophy, which calls for consistent placement and presentation of items throughout the chain but allows for modifications to address differences in purchasing behavior at individual stores. Under this philosophy, items are placed and presented based on attributes such as brand manufacturer, subcategory, type, count, physical size, package color and shape, as well as profit and movement data.

The category manager next programs his shelf-space management system with the placement and presentation requirements for the shampoo category. The system will use these as guidelines in developing planograms automatically. He requires that the category be broken into two subcategories— premium, which includes brands such as Elegance, and budget, which includes brands such as Bargain Bubbles. Within each subcategory, items then are to be merchandised further by brand.

Retailers Checking Out New Ways to Do Business

· · · · · · · · · · · · · · · · ·

The category manager next instructs the program to break down the presentation within brands to position shampoos on the left. Within these types, items are to be arranged from left to right by size, from smallest to largest.

After the general merchandising pattern has been described to the system, these data are merged with fixture measurements for the category, product-assortment data, store-specific customer demand data modified based on demographic potential, and the marketing and financial goals for the category. Integrating these data, the system proceeds to produce store-specific planograms automatically.

Despite Debonair's recommendation that Bargain Bubbles be given horizontal shelf space on one shelf at eye level, the category manager decides that the three brands projected to generate the greatest profit and movement, including Bargain Bubbles, should be given prime eye-level shelf space and displayed vertically on the second and third shelves from the top. The decision reflects his analysis of category profit and movement data by brand (see chart 2.30) and his conclusion that although Bargain Bubbles deserves more and better shelf space, the potential of the other top brands merits equal play for them.

2.30 Brand Sales Analysis

Brand	# of facings	Sales	% Sales	Sales/lin.	Profit
Silky Style	9	$2,850.90	6.4	$9,502.59	$916.37
Elegance	9	$1,985.31	4.4	$5,334.84	$490.20
Bargain Bubbles	27	$1,983.76	4.4	$5,668.92	$374.09
Clean & Soft	39	$18,552.60	41.3	$21,945.44	$4,316.39
1st Impressions	17	$4,808.99	10.7	$13,413.50	$113.33
Mane Tame	16	$4,116.29	9.1	$11,907.67	$847.22

Source: Nielsen Marketing Research, SPACEMAN

Although SuperProfit Foods has not adhered strictly to Debonair's recommendations, the interaction between the chain and the manufacturer promises to improve the category and has resulted in better positioning for Bargain Bubbles—a true "win-win" outcome.

The shelf-space management system now can be programmed to follow this process automatically for each store and for each category within a store to produce store-specific planograms that:

- Maximize item allocation by eliminating wasted space and displaying high-ranked items at the best positions.

- Minimize out-of-stocks.

- Reduce inventory while maximizing profit and customer satisfaction.

Store-specific planograms are crucial to the successful implementation of category management because they integrate all merchandising activities into an actionable plan for the stores—which are the only places the product, the customer, the supplier's marketing plan, and the retailer's merchandising and marketing plans meet.

Retailers Checking Out New Ways to Do Business

• • • • • • • • • • • • • • • •   After the shelf has been set, the shelf-space management system continually measures the performance of planograms against SuperProfit Foods' shampoo category objectives and produces new planograms for each SuperProfit Foods store type (see chart 2.31). It automatically removes from the planogram items that don't meet case-sales criteria and then adjusts shelf quantities to alleviate understock conditions. It also alerts the category manager to slow moving items that he might want to delist to make room for better-performing items that are understocked.

2.31 Financial Analysis—Shampoo Category

	Current	Target
Projected sales	$469.68	$466.59
Lost sales	$8.17	$11.26
Projected GP	$103.18	$102.50
Lost GP	$1.74	$2.42
Projected GP ROII	9.54	11.26
Shelf inventory	$722.75	$610.54
BR inventory	$0.00	$0.00
Store inventory	$722.75	$610.54
Projected turns	33.91	39.88

Source: Nielsen Marketing Research, SPACEMAN

In addition, it prints out schematic reports and other information that the category manager sends to SuperProfit Foods stores as he begins the fourth stage of category management, implementing strategy.

4. Implementing Strategy

After planning his merchandising strategy, the category manager and his specialists must communicate the strategy and related tactics to store managers. They, in turn, must disseminate instructions to store employees, who perform the hands-on work involved with product sorting, pricing changes, display assembly and other tasks.

In this case, the SuperProfit Foods category manager is especially concerned about communications with his Middle Income Families stores, where the most far-reaching and potentially most significant merchandising changes are planned. He must ensure that:

- Items slated for delisting are marked down to hasten sell-through and then eventually removed from the shelves.

- Other items—such as the additional 16-ounce size of Bargain Bubbles—are added and ordered.

- Bargain Bubbles promotions are communicated and handled properly.

- Prices are changed to reflect SuperProfit Foods' new everyday lower pricing strategy.

- Shelf-space allocations are realigned to give Bargain Bubbles a prime location.

Retailers Checking Out New Ways to Do Business

Planogram schematics showing where each product belongs on the shelf are sent from SuperProfit Foods headquarters to individual stores (see chart 2.32). Store managers also receive with each planogram a report that identifies how each product should appear on the shelf (see chart 2.33). The report includes the number of facings and units for each product; it also spells out how many units deep and high the product can go.

2.32 Shampoo Planogram for Middle Income Families Stores

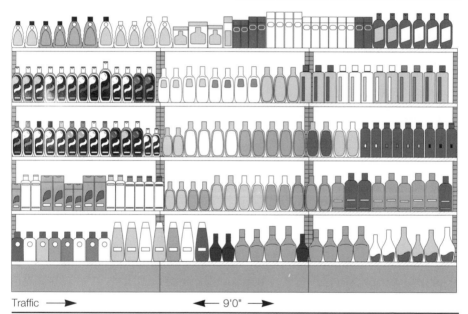

Traffic ⟶   ⟵ 9'0" ⟶

Source: Nielsen Marketing Research, SPACEMAN

2.33 Shampoo Products—Shelf Positions

Name	Number of Facings	Number of Units
Shelf 3 Segment 1		
Bargain Bubbles X-B Lq.15 oz.	2	14
Bargain Bubbles O Lq.16 oz.	2	14
Bargain Bubbles SF Lq.16 oz.	1	7
Bargain Bubbles DF N-O Lot. 16 oz.	1	7
Bargain Bubbles ND Lq. 16 oz.	1	7
Bargain Bubbles STR Lq. 16 oz.	1	8
Bargain Bubbles MS X-B Lq. 16 oz.	1	7
Bargain Bubbles MS Lq. 16 oz.	1	7
Bargain Bubbles X-B Lq. 16 oz.	1	7
Bargain Bubbles B-N Lq. 16 oz.	1	7
Bargain Bubbles X-B Lq. 12 oz.	1	8
Bargain Bubbles ND Lq. 12 oz.	1	8
Shelf 3 Segment 2		
Clean & Soft D Lq. 11 oz.	2	18
Clean & Soft N Lq. 15 oz.	4	32
Clean & Soft O Lq. 15 oz.	5	40
Clean & Soft X-B Lq. 15 oz.	2	16
Shelf 3 Segment 3		
Clean & Soft GTL Lq. 22 oz.	2	12
Elegance X-B Lq. 15 oz.	2	14
Elegance ND Lq. 15 oz.	2	14
Elegance O Lq. 15 oz.	2	14
Elegance CD Lq. 15 oz.	2	14
Elegance MS Lq. 15 oz.	1	7

Source: Nielsen Marketing Research, SPACEMAN

Using the price modeling software program, the category manager generates a price change file that can be key-entered or uploaded to SuperProfit Foods' mainframe computer for inclusion with the retailer's price maintenance system. These changes are then sent to individual stores for implementation.

Chapter 2

Retailers Checking Out New Ways to Do Business

· · · · · · · · · · · · · · · · ·

The promotion planning software program enables the category manager to generate another report outlining promotional plans for individual brands. (see chart 2.34). The report, which is sent to store managers and department managers, enables them to estimate the quantities they'll need of the promoted products and to plan in-store support. The report identifies regular and feature price by store type, recommended in-store display treatment, ad treatment, and in-store signage to be provided to stores. It also includes merchandising comments, if any, for each promoted item.

2.34 Promotion Plans
Store Report: General Merchandise—Zone 1

Health and Beauty Care

Description	Pack	Size	Regular retail	Sale retail w/ coupon	Ad	Coup.	Amt.	Disp.	Sign size
Healthy Multi Vitamins	12	200 ct.	$3.99	$2.99	qtr.			wing	
Fresh Mouthwash	6	32 oz.	$4.59	2/$4.59	qtr.	B1G1	0.00	endl.	
Relief Extra Strength Caplets	6	100 ct.	$6.99	$4.99	qtr.			endl.	
Bargain Bubbles X-B	6	16 oz.	$1.49	$1.09	qtr.			endl.	8X12 *
Bargain Bubbles D	6	16 oz.	$1.49	$1.09	qtr.			endl.	8X12
Bargain Bubbles H R	6	16 oz.	$1.49	$1.09	qtr.			endl.	8X12
Bargain Bubbles N-O	6	16 oz.	$1.49	$1.09	qtr.			endl.	8X12
Bargain Bubbles SF	6	16 oz.	$1.49	$1.09	qtr.			endl.	8X12
Bargain Bubbles MS R	6	16 oz.	$1.49	$1.09	qtr.			endl.	8X12
Bargain Bubbles SFT	6	16 oz.	$1.49	$1.09	qtr.			endl.	8X12
Bargain Bubbles STR	6	16 oz.	$1.49	$1.09	qtr.			endl.	8X12
Bargain Bubbles P ND	6	16 oz.	$1.49	$1.09	qtr.			endl.	8X12
Bargain Bubbles O	6	16 oz.	$1.49	$1.09	qtr.			endl.	8X12
Bargain Bubbles B N	6	16 oz.	$1.49	$1.09	qtr.			endl.	8X12

Source: Nielsen Marketing Research, Nielsen Promotion Management System
* P-O-P for all stores

Because the shelf-space management software program is updated with the purchase behavior of specific demographic clusters, movement data, and other information, the category manager can monitor the progress of the Middle Income Families planogram and send updated planograms and reports with stocking instructions to SuperProfit

Foods' Middle Income Families stores. These planograms reflect product-mix adjustments, and the stocking reports tell store managers and department managers how to re-set product positioning, facings and units within the shampoo category.

5. Evaluating Results

The same software applications that helped the category manager with the first four stages of category management also provide an assist in the final stage of the process, evaluating results.

Getting comprehensive and accurate data rapidly is critical at this stage, because it allows the category manager to react quickly to unforeseen challenges or opportunities in the marketplace.

The scanning-data analyses that provided much of the data for reviewing the category help the category manager gauge the sales and market-share impact of his marketing and merchandising strategies.

He can determine, for instance, whether SuperProfit Foods was successful in halting and/or regaining lost sales and market share from other chains and outlets, particularly mass merchandisers. He also can ascertain whether pricing, promotion and product mix helped to boost brand and category volume. In addition, he'll be able to tell how Bargain Bubbles performed and how it contributed to the category's performance. This information will help to measure the value of SuperProfit Foods and Debonair working together and sharing data resources.

Using the demographic and purchase-behavior database that enabled him to identify his target consumers, the category manager can determine whether SuperProfit Foods succeeded in attracting the targeted consumers from other retail outlets. He

Retailers Checking Out New Ways to Do Business

• • • • • • • • • • • • • • • • • •

also can see who is buying shampoo at the chain, how often, and how much they're spending. In addition, he can gauge the effect of new Middle Income Families buyers on the category.

The price modeling program that allowed the category manager to test various pricing strategies now lets him answer a number of key questions about the strategy he ultimately selected. Did SuperProfit Foods achieve target gross margins for the category and the department? Did other categories pick up the shampoo category's gross-margin slack? Did the chain, in fact, become more price-competitive with mass merchandisers and other competitors? Through consumer research, SuperProfit Foods also can determine how its new shampoo pricing strategy has affected its image.

Meanwhile, the promotion planning system helps the category manager compare projected sales and profits with actual results for specific promotions.

The shelf-space management program allows him to monitor constantly how the category and individual brands are progressing toward objectives. The shelf-space system also can help him evaluate the allocation of shelf space from the category level down to the item level to find out whether the chain is meeting sales and profitability goals, achieving desired service levels, and whether it's optimizing its space requirements by controlling inventory levels and limiting out-of-stocks and overstocks.

All of this feedback enables the category manager to identify challenges and opportunities in the marketplace and to begin planning his response. This leads him naturally back into the first stage of category management, reviewing the category. It's a step he always must take before changing course — even a little bit. By starting over, he closes the category management loop and ensures that each new decision he makes will be well-informed, timely and relevant to marketplace conditions.

CHAPTER 3

Manufacturers
Looking For Ways To
Turn Up The Volume

Manufacturers Looking for Ways to Turn Up the Volume

In the business world, as in the world of nature, it's not hard to tell when the seasons are changing.

Although the signs might not be as noisy as a thunderclap, or as physically discomforting as a sharp drop in temperature, they are no less recognizable.

Consider, for example, the changing role of the manufacturer in the consumer packaged goods marketplace.

Not too many years ago, manufacturers were the leaders of the marketplace, and retailers were their distribution arms. Manufacturers knew the marketplace well, and retailers were content to rely on their marketing wisdom.

Those were the simpler days of mass marketing, when manufacturers used national advertising in general-interest magazines, on network TV and on AM radio to build brand equity.

During the last 20 years, however, many developments have brought this era to an end. Demographic and socioeconomic trends have shattered the marketplace into countless fragments, increasing the need for target-marketing, while consolidation among retailers has left fewer chains and independents to sell manufacturers' products, increasing the importance of each distribution opportunity.

3.1A

At the same time, a blurring of retail trade channels has made defining distribution opportunities more complex. No longer are there just food stores, drug stores or mass merchandisers. The marketplace also includes food/drug "combos," "super-combos," warehouse stores and wholesale clubs, among a variety of other formats, many of which carry similar products. Food stores are selling drugs, drug stores are selling food, and mass merchandisers are selling both.

The proliferation of store types has made competition more intense than ever among retailers, leading many to become marketers themselves. Aided by advances in technology, applications and information, they are striving to customize their stores to meet specific consumer needs and to differentiate themselves from the competition. With retailers becoming better positioned to reach the marketplace, manufacturers have seen their information and marketing edge fade (see figures 3.1A and 3.1B).

3.1B

Consumers have changed, too. Faced with numerous shopping options, and recognizing the intense price competition that exists among retailers, today's shopper is more likely than ever to cherry-pick among stores—and among brands. Market research, in fact, shows that two-thirds of purchase decisions are now made in store aisles. This trend, coupled with marketplace fragmentation, has created a growing need for manufacturers to ensure effective merchandising and promotion of their products at the store level, while still building brand equity nationwide.

These developments have ushered in a new era in the consumer packaged goods marketplace, one in which the manufacturer's role and the manufacturer-retailer relationship have changed dramatically. The former manufacturer-retailer relationship has given way to strategic alliances in which manufacturers and retailers share their knowledge to achieve their individual marketing objectives.

There is no surer sign of the dramatic change in the manufacturer's role than the steady increase during the last 10 years in annual trade promotion expenditures as a percentage of manufacturers' total advertising and promotion budgets.

Manufacturers Looking for Ways to Turn Up the Volume

Today, the average manufacturer spends 50 percent of his advertising and promotion budget on trade promotions, and trade promotion spending amounts to an average of 11 percent of the gross revenues for most brands (see chart 3.2).

3.2 Ad and Trade Promotion Expenditure Importance

Share of expenditures by type

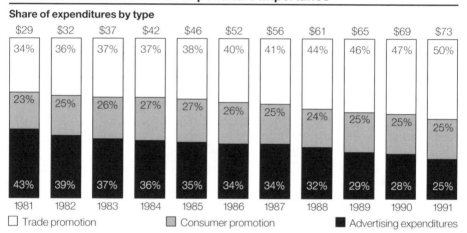

	$29	$32	$37	$42	$46	$52	$56	$61	$65	$69	$73
Trade promotion	34%	36%	37%	37%	38%	40%	41%	44%	46%	47%	50%
Consumer promotion	23%	25%	26%	27%	27%	26%	25%	24%	25%	25%	25%
Advertising expenditures	43%	39%	37%	36%	35%	34%	34%	32%	29%	28%	25%
	1981	1982	1983	1984	1985	1986	1987	1988	1989	1990	1991

☐ Trade promotion ☐ Consumer promotion ■ Advertising expenditures

Source: Nielsen Marketing Research, Donnelley Marketing

The increased spending on trade promotions, which often comes at the expense of media and consumer promotions, is going toward merchandising incentives for retailers, such as off-invoice allowances, co-op dollars, consignment purchasing, special terms and creative market development funds.

In essence, manufacturers are looking at trade promotion spending as a strategy for providing a short-term lift in volume and not necessarily as a way to enhance brand equity.

Eager to enhance narrow profit margins, retailers have welcomed this increased trade promotion spending, viewing it as a way to reduce costs. The change has dovetailed particularly well with the objectives of "power retailers" that have emerged as the result of the many mergers, acquisitions and leveraged buyouts among retailers in recent years. Often faced with great pressure to meet stringent financial goals, power retailers view trade promotions as a way to meet their immediate financial needs.

Manufacturers' and retailers' increased reliance on trade promotions isn't the only sign that a new era has arrived in the consumer packaged goods marketplace.

Another telling development is the decision by many manufacturers and retailers to adopt a completely new process for marketing and selling their products in the 1990s—a process that puts them in closer touch with the tastes and needs of shoppers at individual stores.

Known as category management, this process involves managing product categories as individual business units and customizing each category's product mix, merchandising and promotions according to customer preference on a store-by-store basis.

This process is fostering within manufacturing companies the development of a team approach to selling that is breaking down communications barriers among sales, marketing, research and MIS departments and is leading to enhanced operational efficiencies.

It also is helping manufacturers respond effectively to their two greatest challenges in the 1990s: Understanding consumers better and building long-term, mutually beneficial relationships with retailers.

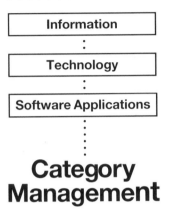

Information
Technology
Software Applications

Category Management

Chapter 3

Manufacturers Looking for Ways to Turn Up the Volume

Category Management Capitalizes on Information Explosion

Category management has been made possible by the continuing development of three important tools: technology, applications and information. Advances in technology (such as electronic check-out scanners) are generating unprecedented amounts of market data, which, through software applications (such as personal-computer programs for analyzing pricing, promotions and shelf space by category) coalesce into information.

Twenty years ago, just having such information would have given any manufacturer or retailer a major competitive advantage. Today, it's not having the information that matters. It's how you use it. And a growing number of manufacturers and retailers are recognizing that they can use it most effectively by implementing category management—and then working together to maximize its benefits.

With market forces pulling manufacturers and retailers closer together, category management provides a common framework to support the development of long-term, mutually beneficial relationships.

The philosophical foundation for the process involves the notion that manufacturers and retailers are powerful marketing enterprises that can attain their individual marketing and financial objectives more easily by cooperating and sharing knowledge with each other.

The manufacturer is concerned primarily with building brand image and brand equity. The retailer wants to build an image as a company that meets specific consumer needs. Both parties, of course, want to increase volume and profitability. By working together through the process of category management, each party can help the other achieve its goals.

Manufacturer   Retailer

102

Retailers, for example, might have access to more market information than ever, but often don't have the time to analyze it thoroughly to identify significant consumer and category trends. Many still rely on manufacturers for expertise and guidance in this regard. It's common for retailers to appoint a savvy manufacturer as the "captain" for a particular category and then to rely on that manufacturer for category insights and strategic recommendations that can boost volume and profitability.

Manufacturers, on the other hand, might have extensive information about brand performance, but they might not be aware of certain nuances of consumer behavior or competitive activity at individual stores. Retailers can help them fill in these blanks by sharing local-market intelligence.

Building close relationships with retailers through category management enhances a manufacturer's ability to target merchandising and promotions to individual stores.

Evolution of Manufacturers' Role Makes Old Ways of Doing Business Extinct

Just as changing seasons cause people to wear different clothes, changing business relationships require business people to adapt to new roles and new challenges.

No one knows this better than the people who work in manufacturers' sales organizations. The manufacturer's changing role in the consumer packaged goods marketplace has created a mountain of challenges for these people to climb.

Increased trade spending has left many sales managers facing short-term goals that conflict with long-term marketing strategies aimed at building and preserving brand franchises.

Chapter 3

Manufacturers Looking for Ways to Turn Up the Volume

• • • • • • • • • • • • • •

The steady increase in trade promotions and associated retail deals has spawned an entire class of shoppers who wait to purchase products when they are on promotion.

Complicating matters further, sales managers must contend with a new breed of price-conditioned shoppers and a new breed of sophisticated retailers.

The steady increase in trade promotions and associated retail deals has spawned an entire class of shoppers who wait to purchase products when they are on promotion.

At the same time, many retailers now promote their own store logos as a brand, a strategy that may or may not conflict with the interests of manufacturers, who have struggled to build and preserve their own brand franchises. This trend has shifted retailers' focus from individual-brand performance to the impact of merchandising and promotional tactics on entire product categories and on the retailer's overall image.

Retailers have continued to differentiate themselves by using various store formats; generating more targeted media and discounting rather than relying on manufacturers' brands or specials; and merchandising products more selectively in certain clusters of stores.

Many retailers also have bolstered their advertising presence, relative to manufacturers, by using the same tools that manufacturers traditionally have employed, such as couponing and advertising on television and radio. Recognizing the impact of marketplace fragmentation and changing consumer lifestyles, they increasingly are aiming their marketing efforts at specific types of consumers, using targeted strategies such as direct-mail videos, point-of-sale advertising, and frequent shopper mailings. Some retailers even have moved away from using newspapers, their traditional vehicle for promotional advertising.

Category management enables the manufacturer's sales organization to address these and other challenges by providing a way to sort through the voluminous data now available about category and brand performance and to extract the information that will support their sales story when they approach the retailer.

Through category management, the manufacturer's sales organization not only can demonstrate its brands' ability to produce profitable volume for a retailer, but also can build the brands' volume, franchise and profits for the manufacturer.

The sales organization, however, cannot realize the benefits of category management by itself. To implement category management successfully, the manufacturer must create an environment in which the members of its organization combine efforts and function as a team.

Adopting Team Approach Fosters Growth

Until recently, manufacturers viewed the functions and responsibilities of the sales department as different and separate from those of marketing and marketing research (see chart 3.3).

Sales managers, whose primary focus always has been the retailer, had a volume responsibility. They concentrated on gaining distribution, strengthening in-store presence and achieving greater merchandising support from the retailer. They also fought for more immediate trade payments to increase short-term case volume.

The marketing department's main responsibility was to focus on consumers in producing ongoing, profitable volume. Marketers concentrated on product development, packaging, media advertising, consumer and trade promotions, price points

Category management provides a way to sort through the voluminous data and to extract the information that will support their sales story when they approach the retailer.

Manufacturers Looking for Ways to Turn Up the Volume

3.3 Traditional Manufacturer Marketing/ Sales Organization Responsibilities

and distribution opportunities. They also fought for long-run brand equity and profits by often using heavy media advertising.

As category management has taken root among manufacturers, it has become more common for marketing, marketing research, sales, and information systems management to work together as a unified team. In fact, the responsibilities of sales teams are becoming more closely aligned with marketing and marketing research.

Marketing departments recognize that retailers are gaining power and becoming their full-fledged marketing partners. They also see that escalating trade promotion budgets are leaving fewer promotional dollars for media exposure and consumer promotions, which is threatening their ability to build their brand franchise and profit responsibilities in the traditional sense.

3.4 Evolving Manufacturer Organization

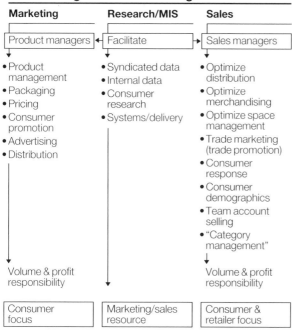

Marketing	Research/MIS	Sales
Product managers	Facilitate	Sales managers
• Product management • Packaging • Pricing • Consumer promotion • Advertising • Distribution	• Syndicated data • Internal data • Consumer research • Systems/delivery	• Optimize distribution • Optimize merchandising • Optimize space management • Trade marketing (trade promotion) • Consumer response • Consumer demographics • Team account selling • "Category management"
Volume & profit responsibility		Volume & profit responsibility
Consumer focus	Marketing/sales resource	Consumer & retailer focus

These realities demand that manufacturers improve their understanding of consumer needs and become more flexible with promotional programs so they not only achieve the manufacturer's objectives, but also complement the retailer's strategies and franchise-building efforts.

As a result, marketing departments are working more closely with sales managers to preserve their brand franchise (see chart 3.4).

In many instances, marketing research is now funneling consumer research information to sales managers, who are relying more on such information in their dealings with specific retail customers (see chart 3.4).

Chapter 3

Manufacturers Looking for Ways to Turn Up the Volume

Instead of concentrating on their own brands, sales managers now are responsible for assessing entire categories and determining their impact on other categories by analyzing scanning, promotion, demographic and other information. In the past, this responsibility belonged only to the brand manager.

While the relationship between marketing and sales departments is changing, an evolution also is taking place in the role of sales managers, who are moving from their volume-oriented mentality of the 1970s toward becoming full-fledged business managers seeking to build brand franchises and produce profitable volume consistent with brand-management goals.

Instead of rewarding sales managers solely on the basis of volume attainment, leading manufacturers have established bonus programs that revolve around profit responsibility (see chart 3.4).

To achieve profitable volume, sophisticated sales managers no longer focus simply on persuasive selling skills and building a rapport with retailers. Rather, they concentrate on tailoring promotion strategies for specific retail accounts in addition to consumer needs. They negotiate promotional programs and price points with retailers, whom they perceive as marketing partners, and they attempt to identify mutually beneficial strategies.

Instead of concentrating on their own brands, sales managers now are responsible for assessing entire categories and determining their impact on other categories by analyzing scanning, promotion, demographic and other information. In the past, this responsibility belonged only to the brand manager.

The sales manager of the '90s wants a better understanding of his customer—the retailer—who already has been examining category interrelationships.

The evolving roles of sales and brand managers demand that they understand changes in retailer strategy, including the retailer's effort to become a neighborhood marketer.

Blurring Roles Create Clearer Vision on How to Increase Sales

With sales and marketing working together as a team to achieve their common goals of growing their brand franchise and producing profitable volume, they seem to act more like each other every day. For example, retailer space management, which has been primarily a focus of sales, now has been added to marketing managers' vocabulary.

It also has become more difficult to distinguish between the roles of brand and sales managers in the area of strategic planning. Team selling involving marketing research and sales managers has become common in today's marketplace. The most sophisticated manufacturers also are involving finance, logistical distribution and food brokers in their new strategic efforts to market through the retailer.

While the roles of brand and sales managers are becoming more intertwined, manufacturers also are creating new positions, including trade promotion manager, trade marketing manager, category manager and product sales managers.

With category management leading to new job titles and revised job descriptions, manufacturers must tackle the issues of education and training within their restructured organizations to compete effectively in a more sophisticated marketplace.

Both sales and brand managers, for example, must cultivate new skills. Both must be effective business managers. They also must possess category expertise and enhanced consumer knowledge. And they must be able to communicate and work with other departments.

Manufacturers Looking for Ways to Turn Up the Volume

• • • • • • • • • • • • • • • •

To augment their education, managers frequently are turning to technological advancements made in recent years. Designed for ease of use and to meet sales and marketing needs, today's sophisticated equipment, data and analyses can help managers tackle their jobs with enhanced skills.

The manufacturer's changing role in the consumer packaged goods marketplace has challenged the developers of technology and applications to keep pace with new sales and marketing needs.

For example, manufacturers' information systems management personnel, as well as research, marketing and sales departments, have a growing need to combine internal data, such as statistics on shipments and financial data, with syndicated data, such as scanning and consumer information.

Sales and brand managers also are depending increasingly on technology to manage the increased amount of data now available on an account-by-account basis. Today, account-specific information is collected from retailers representing about 50 percent of the total of all commodity volume (ACV) available to consumer packaged goods manufacturers. The goal is to replace paper reports with sophisticated application analyses that concentrate on distribution, promotion, pricing and space-management opportunities.

As technology and applications continue to develop, information systems and delivery vehicles seem to be moving away from headquarters installations and into the hands of sales and brand managers, who are using them to address the needs of retail customers.

A toolbox approach is developing that allows sales and brand managers to access the knowledge they need at the level that meets their demands. Sales force automation not only can enhance field productivity, but also can guide business management decision-making through increased knowledge and communications.

Category Management Helps Develop the Big Picture

Category management helps manufacturers put this abundance of information in perspective, while meeting the ever-increasing requirements of the marketplace.

In essence, it permits manufacturers to be more efficient at marketing and working with the retailer. Through category management, manufacturers can bring an expanded knowledge base to retailers for their use and for the individual benefit of both parties. This enables manufacturers to display their commitment to their retail customers' success.

Manufacturers Looking for Ways to Turn Up the Volume

The Five Stages of Category Management

Category management is an ongoing, dynamic process that involves managing categories as separate businesses, each with its own pricing and profit/loss responsibilities. The manufacturer can undertake this new selling/marketing approach most successfully by focusing on five important stages. They include:

1. Reviewing the category
2. Targeting consumers
3. Planning merchandising
4. Implementing strategy
5. Evaluating results

Before putting these stages in motion, the manufacturer first must define a category. This isn't as easy as it might sound, because retailers and market research companies sometimes view a category differently than manufacturers, and shoppers sometimes have yet another definition.

When in doubt, the manufacturer always should err on the side of the consumer, including in a category any products that, from a consumer point of view, could be substituted for one another. Third-party data can help manufacturers get a handle on consumer perceptions of a category.

In defining a category, the manufacturer should identify key subcategories that can significantly influence the performance of the category as a whole. For example, within the dentrifice category, a manufacturer would want to recognize subcategories such as "pump" toothpastes and baking-soda-based toothpastes.

The manufacturer should understand the trends that drive each subcategory and should determine the impact the subcategory has on other products—in the same category and across categories. Similarly, the manufacturer should understand how one category's performance can affect another's. For example, the fortunes of the beverage and snacks categories often are intertwined.

Having defined a category, a manufacturer can proceed with the five stages of category management.

The first stage, reviewing the category, requires that a manufacturer gather and integrate a broad range of internal and external data to create a national overview of the category.

Essential pieces of information include the category's unit and dollar volume and growth rates, both on a national basis and by retail trade

Reviewing the Category

Manufacturers Looking for Ways to Turn Up the Volume

channel; the level of advertising and promotional activity within the category; and the number of new products introduced into the category during the last year.

The manufacturer also should examine national household purchasing patterns, including how many households buy products from the category, where they shop and how much they spend.

It's also important for the manufacturer to chart the performance of its brands versus those of competitors at the national, market and retail-account levels. The manufacturer would want to answer questions such as:

• What are my brands' market shares versus the competition?

• How are they faring in terms of dollar volume and profitability?

• If my brand isn't the category's market share leader, whose is, and by how much?

• Which products are trending up, and which ones are declining, both across the category and within its subcategories?

• How do consumer and trade promotions affect the performance of specific products and the category as a whole?

• How do retail accounts stack up in terms of category market share?

• How do specific accounts handle product mix, pricing, promotion and shelf space for my brands and the category as a whole?

• How does this category affect other categories, and vice versa?

• Are there cross-merchandising or cross-promotion opportunities between this category and others?

The answers to these questions, coupled with other data collected during the category review, will enable the manufacturer to identify growth opportunities and to capitalize on them by developing new or modified marketing strategies.

Through the next stage of category management, targeting consumers, the manufacturer can tailor its strategies based on the needs of specific types of consumers.

Targeting Consumers

This stage involves three steps:

1) Building a demographic profile of the typical buyer, both for the category and for a specific brand. The profile would include information such as income level, family size and age. It also would indicate whether the typical buyer purchased a lot or a little, where the purchases usually occurred, whether the typical buyer was price-sensitive, and whether he was likely to use coupons.

2) Identifying and evaluating target groups. This step involves analyzing general information about the lifestyles of target consumers. What products do they buy? What stores do they shop at? What leisure activities do they pursue? This information can yield a deeper understanding of the needs of target customers. It also can help a manufacturer identify cross-merchandising opportunities and can provide useful knowledge for the development of advertising aimed at target consumers.

3) Planning promotion and media strategies. By examining data on consumer media preferences, the manufacturer can select the appropriate advertising vehicles, such as television, radio, magazines and newspapers, for reaching target consumers. For instance, are they watching news-oriented television shows? Or do they prefer reading health magazines?

Manufacturers Looking for Ways to Turn Up the Volume

• • • • • • • • • • • • • • • • •

By matching the consumer profile of a brand to a profile of consumers within the trade areas of individual stores, a manufacturer can determine not only a brand's potential within a specific store, but also the potential for a brand's buyers to improve category performance at a particular site. The manufacturer also can determine the most effective product mix, pricing, promotion and merchandising for doing so.

Planning Merchandising

The third stage of category management, planning merchandising, involves developing a detailed strategy by retail account for product mix, pricing, promotion, and shelf-space allocation within a category.

In examining product mix, a manufacturer can use software applications to determine which of its brands a particular retailer does not carry and which of these have strong volume potential for both the retailer and the manufacturer.

These applications also enable a manufacturer to recommend an optimum product mix by projecting the volume and profit gains a retailer would realize by adding such items to its product mix and delisting other items. By making such recommendations, a manufacturer can demonstrate its category knowledge to the retailer. However, the manufacturer's credibility will depend largely on

The manufacturer must be familiar with the retailer

- *Image*
- *Market strategy*
- *Premier, high-low or everyday low-price*
- *Financial & marketing objectives*

its willingness to avoid recommendations biased toward its own brands. A manufacturer, for instance, should not recommend that only competitors' items be delisted and only its items be added.

When trying to determine appropriate pricing and promotion strategies for a category, a manufacturer must recognize that retailers design specific promotional programs for each store or cluster of stores, and that the manufacturer's brand or brands are only part of the entire category. Both the retailer and manufacturer must focus on the category as a whole to execute mutually beneficial pricing and promotional strategies.

To accomplish this, the manufacturer must become familiar with the retailer's image and overall marketing strategy. Is the retailer a premier, high-low, or everyday low-price outlet? What are the financial and marketing objectives for each category and product grouping?

Retailers develop their pricing strategy to address profitability, price image, and competition. Today's sophisticated technology enables retailers to evaluate the effect a pricing strategy will have on gross margins for an entire store, a department, a category or individual items. Manufacturers must be aware of the retailer's use of pricing in establishing an image and building a consumer franchise within the market.

The best pricing deal is one that produces savings for the consumer and offers profit for both the manufacturer and retailer. Deal profitability models test different merchandising scenarios from the retailer's perspective and the manufacturer's perspective to develop a mutually beneficial strategy. Key variables, such as FSIs, seasonality, holidays, deal terms and allowances, forward buying and shelf space, also are built into the model.

Deal profitability models test different merchandising scenarios from the retailer's perspective...

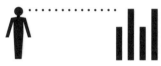

and the manufacturer's perspective...

to develop a mutually beneficial strategy.

Manufacturers Looking for Ways to Turn Up the Volume

Another component of planning merchandising is producing planograms that show exactly how and where products should be displayed on the shelf within a category at individual stores.

Sophisticated software applications enable the manufacturer to assist the retailer in customizing planograms for specific types of stores, so that each store stocks more of the products that appeal to people in its trade area and fewer of those items that lack appeal.

These applications allow the manufacturer to segment stores based on the type of consumers in their trade areas, and then to create customized planograms for each segment, taking into account variables such as customer demographics, the size and type of fixturing, inventory requirements, and a retailer's merchandising philosophy. In addition, information about pricing, promotions and product movement can be factored in to determine whether specific merchandising strategies will allow the manufacturer and retailer to achieve their volume and profit goals.

Because these applications are automated, planograms can be created within hours to match various strategic store clusters without manually repeating the process for each planogram, a task that used to take days. Productivity can be expanded beyond usual work hours, because once the applications program is given instructions, it can perform functions without human intervention.

Shelf-space management applications also issue inventory replenishment schedules for like items within a planogram so a manufacturer can better time its shipments to a retailer—a must in an environment in which retailers are relying increasingly on just-in-time delivery.

By assisting in the development of category-wide shelf-space management strategies, the manufacturer can help the retailer ensure that the right products are in the right stores in the right quantity at the right time. In doing so, the manufacturer can establish itself as a "category captain" whom the retailer relies on for market insights and recommendations.

Implementing Strategy

The first major test for any category marketing and merchandising strategy comes during the fourth stage of category management, implementing strategy.

At this point, the manufacturer's team sales leader makes his presentation to the category buyer at the retail account for which the strategy was devised.

Using information gleaned during the first three stages of the category management process, the team sales leader provides an overview of the category, his brands and consumer purchasing patterns.

He then delivers his recommendations about product mix, pricing, promotions and shelf-space strategies, supporting his case with charts, tables, planograms and other output from analyses conducted as he planned merchandising for the category. For example, he might use tables produced by a modeling system to show how pricing and promotion strategies for one of his brands will affect the brand itself as well as the performance of the category as a whole.

He relates these recommendations to the demographics of the retailer's target customers and to the retailer's financial objectives, explaining how the proposed strategies will help the retailer attract more customers to its stores and improve category volume and profits.

Manufacturers Looking for Ways to Turn Up the Volume

● ● ● ● ● ● ● ● ● ● ● ● ● ● ● ●

Implementing strategy isn't confined to one presentation to a retail buyer. It's a long process that requires a continuing dialogue between the manufacturer and the retailer.

In discussing promotions, the manufacturer should note opportunities to tie together promotions across categories, and to take maximum advantage of special allowances provided by the manufacturer. Leading-edge manufacturers have begun to sign one-year contracts stipulating the amount in special allowances a retailer will receive over a 12-month period, with the understanding that the manufacturer and retailer will try to tie their promotions together.

The team sales leader also describes national brand advertising plans, explaining how the manufacturer plans to use media-preference data to direct its message to target consumers. In doing this, it's important that the team sales leader emphasize the indirect, local benefit for the retailer that accrues from national advertising targeted at specific consumer groups. It demonstrates yet another way that the manufacturer is helping the retailer while also pursuing national brand-building strategies.

Implementing strategy isn't confined to one presentation to a retail buyer. It's a long process that requires a continuing dialogue between the manufacturer and the retailer.

After implementing merchandising and marketing strategies for a category, the manufacturer next must evaluate their impact.

Evaluating Results

This fifth stage of category management is as critical to the process as pedals are to a bicycle.

That's because it involves questions, answers and decisions that keep the circular process flowing naturally back into its first stage, reviewing the category.

The basic question to be answered is: "Did my strategies achieve their objectives?"

Today's sophisticated software applications can help manufacturers answer this question and many others. These applications enable manufacturers to convert scanning statistics and other market data into actionable knowledge. And they allow the manufacturer to do this faster than ever. Automated computer systems, in fact, can be programmed to digest large amounts of market data and produce on a regular schedule customized reports on the performance of brands and categories.

This knowledge can help manufacturer's sales managers and brand managers identify new opportunities and unforeseen challenges in the marketplace. They then must decide if and how to modify their strategies. These decisions require managers to review their category once again, providing the link that makes category management a dynamic, ongoing process.

Category Management in Action— a Case in Point

To encourage a better understanding of category management, Nielsen has developed a working example of the five-stage process in action. The example involves a fictitious manufacturer, Debonair, Inc.; a retailer, SuperProfit Foods; and a category, shampoo, including all types and formulas of shampoo.

Debonair is a mid-sized company that manufactures hair-care products and cosmetics. It entered the business with a budget shampoo, Bargain Bubbles, to maximize market share, and later introduced premium-priced products, such as Elegance shampoo, to satisfy upscale customers and to maximize profitability. Debonair is now a market leader in the shampoo category at the national, market and retailer levels.

Manufacturers Looking for Ways to Turn Up the Volume

• • • • • • • • • • • • • • • • SuperProfit Foods is a leading chain in a major metropolitan market. Its full-service, high-end food and drug "combo" stores offer consumers the convenience of one-stop shopping. The chain features a variety of high-quality products at competitive prices but uses promotional pricing as well. The role of the shampoo category at SuperProfit Foods stores is profit generator.

1. Reviewing the Category

To review the shampoo category, Debonair must analyze the category's size, growth and trends, as well as category and brand sales and shares (and changes), product mix, promotion, pricing and shelf space.

Debonair begins its category review by assembling a national overview of the shampoo category. The company learns that the category had more than 2,000 active UPCs nationwide and annual dollar sales of $1.21 billion in all trade outlets during the year studied. The category also exhibited a three percent dollar growth versus the same period a year ago.

Next, Debonair analyzes category sales performance by retail trade channel. The company finds that although supermarkets with sales over $2 million represent 50.5 percent of total dollar sales, 71 percent of all shampoo category buyers use a non-food outlet for at least one of their category purchases during the year. Debonair also discovers another important fact: supermarkets recorded a negligible increase in shampoo sales during the year. This indicates category growth must have come from other outlet types (see charts 3.5A and 3.5B). Further investigation shows that mass merchandisers, representing 24.5 percent of category dollar sales, exhibited a growth rate of 8.1 percent. Drug outlets, which account for 25.0 percent of overall dollar

3.5A Shampoo Dollar Share

Across trade channels

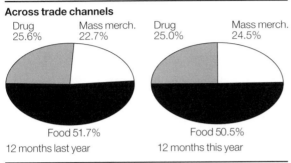

Drug
25.6%

Mass merch.
22.7%

Drug
25.0%

Mass merch.
24.5%

Food 51.7%

Food 50.5%

12 months last year

12 months this year

Source: Nielsen Marketing Research, Procision

3.5B Shampoo Growth

Across trade channels

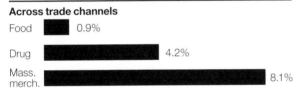

Food   0.9%

Drug   4.2%

Mass. merch.   8.1%

Dollar sales—percent change vs. year-ago

Source: Nielsen Marketing Research, Procision

sales, had a somewhat less significant growth rate of 4.2 percent versus the same period a year ago.

Debonair also learns that shampoo led all HBA (health and beauty aid) categories in promotional activity in supermarkets. Ninety percent of all retailers undertook major feature advertising, and 89 percent displayed the category at least once during the year. Thirty percent of all shampoo items on retail shelves were promoted at least one time.

The company also discovers that shampoo is one of the more active HBA categories for new product introductions. Almost 300 new items were launched during the year at the retail level.

Manufacturers Looking for Ways to Turn Up the Volume

Getting to the Root of Shampoo Sales

Understanding the source of shampoo sales changes requires a knowledge of the dynamics of sales. Sales are a function of penetration—how many households are buying—times the buying rate, or how much the households are purchasing.

So, after putting together a national overview of the shampoo category, Debonair turns its attention to national household purchasing patterns for the shampoo category. Interestingly, the data show that in the overall U.S. market, household penetration declined during the year studied, with three percent fewer households buying shampoo compared with the previous year (see chart 3.6). With this three-point drop in household penetration, 78 percent of the 94.7 million U.S. households purchased shampoo.

The data also show that the three percent increase in dollars expended on shampoo nationally can be traced to the fact that 6 percent more dollars were spent by the average shampoo buyer (see chart 3.6). What's more, the average buyer bought the category at a rate of 5.8 times during the year, purchasing on average 1.3 units on each occasion.

3.6 Consumer Shampoo Sales by Outlet

(Percent dollar change vs. prior period)

	Penetration	Dollars/buyer
All Outlets	-3%	+6%
Food ($4MM+)	+1%	-4%
Drug	-6%	+8%
Mass merchandiser	+3%	+4%

Source: Nielsen Marketing Research, Nielsen Household Services

Each of the 73.8 million households purchasing the shampoo category during the year spent an average of $16.25, an increase of almost a dollar per buyer over the previous year. The average price reported by consumers was $2.17 per unit, an increase of two percent.

The household purchasing data also help Debonair determine where shoppers are buying shampoo. When considering the three primary outlets for shampoo sales—food stores, mass merchandisers and drug stores—Debonair discovers that food and mass merchandisers attracted more buyers, while shampoo customer traffic in drug stores fell by six percent (see chart 3.6). The increase in the number of shampoo consumers within food stores was off-set by a decline in the amount spent by the average buyer on the category. Conversely the average shampoo consumer at drug stores and at mass merchandisers purchased more of the category than their year-ago counterpart.

Analyzing Shampoo Data Can Get Hairy

After analyzing household purchasing patterns for the shampoo category, Debonair continues its review by studying and comparing data that charts the performance of the category as a whole, and of the company's brands, at the national, market and retailer levels. (For the purposes of this example, data from only one representative metropolitan market and one representative retailer—SuperProfit Foods—in that market have been selected. In an actual category review, a manufacturer would review data from many markets and retailers.)

Although the shampoo category showed no significant change nationally in dollar sales for the 12-month period studied, during the most recent

Manufacturers Looking for Ways to Turn Up the Volume

• • • • • • • • • • • • • • • •

quarter—in which sales of $146.9 million were recorded—there was a 4.5 percent decline in dollar sales compared with the same period a year ago.

Debonair discovers that a similar pattern existed at the market level. There was a slight gain in shampoo category dollar sales for the year, but a decline of 3.5 percent for the latest quarter. HBA sales at the market level didn't grow as much in the latest quarter versus the year, partially because of the decline in shampoo sales, which account for six percent of HBA sales. Within the market, in fact, three of the four reporting retailers showed similar losses for the HBA department and shampoo category.

At the retail account level, SuperProfit Foods' shampoo dollar volume was down 19.6 percent in the most recent quarter and down 9.7 percent for the year. The chain's share of shampoo sales declined 3.2 percent from 19.1 percent a year ago. SuperProfit Foods, which has an 18.3 percent share of the market ACV (all commodity volume), is currently responsible for only 15.9 percent of shampoo sales in the market (see chart 3.7). This means the chain is significantly underdeveloped in the shampoo category and is not achieving its "fair share" of dollar volume.

3.7 Brand Ranking

13 weeks

| | SuperProfit Foods (18.3% ACV) | | | | | Market | | | | | |
	Rank	LY rank	Dollar share	Share change	% promo.	Rank	LY rank	Dollar share	Share change	% promo.	Acct. % of market
Shampoo	–	–	–	–	9.9	–	–	–	–	12.8	15.9
Clean & Soft	1	1	13.9	1.1	14.9	1	1	12.6	-0.5	7.8	17.5
1st Impressions	2	2	10.0	-0.9	0.7	3	2	9.1	-1.6	9.0	17.3
Mane Tame	3	5	8.3	3.1	16.7	4	5	6.3	2.1	11.8	20.9
Bargain Bubbles	4	3	7.3	1.2	9.7	2	3	10.0	1.8	27.2	11.6
Silky Style	5	4	5.5	-0.1	5.2	6	4	3.9	-0.8	6.7	22.6
Elegance	6	9	4.0	0.6	14.8	5	7	4.3	0.9	17.3	14.6

Source: Nielsen Marketing Research, Sales Advisor

Through the use of artificial intelligence, Debonair identifies three major factors that are driving these trends.

- First, a comparison of SuperProfit Foods' performance with the market's shows that the retailer is promoting the shampoo category less often and less effectively than competitors. SuperProfit Foods sells 9.9 percent of shampoo on promotion, compared with a market average of 12.8 percent (see chart 3.7). and a national average of 14.5 percent. Furthermore, shampoo volume sold on promotion at SuperProfit Foods declined 4.9 percent versus the same period a year ago.

- Second, SuperProfit Foods sells shampoo at an average of $.31 higher than the rest of the market.

- Third, the retailer is not carrying the appropriate product mix to attract category purchases. Since shampoo is one of the more active categories for new products, the item mix must be continually evaluated to make profitable stocking decisions. Slower-moving items should be delisted to create shelf space for more promising items. Debonair next analyzes the brand's performance at the national, market and retailer levels.

Manufacturers Looking for Ways to Turn Up the Volume

. . . .

Studying Your Brand Name to Make Your Mark

Nationally, Bargain Bubbles performed well versus a year ago, posting a dollar volume increase of 8.2 percent and garnering a 9.9 percent share of the category, up 1.2 share points (see chart 3.8).

3.8 Bargain Bubbles Product Profile

13 Weeks

Shampoo	Current	Year-ago	Change
Volume (MM)	146.9	153.8	-4.5%
% Promo. volume	14.1	14.1	NC
Bargain Bubbles			
Volume (M)	14,487.9	13,388.4	+8.2%
Share	9.9	8.7	+1.2
% Promo. volume	26.7	26.0	+0.7%
Major ad ACV	8	8	NC
Display ACV	21	16	+5
Feat. & disp. ACV	4	4	NC
Price (eq. unit)	6.33	6.32	+0.2%
Distribution	99	99	NC

Source: Nielsen Marketing Research, Spotlight

In the market, Bargain Bubbles ranked second—up from third a year earlier—and showed a large increase in dollar volume of 17.4 percent and an increase of 1.8 share points to a 10.0 share. This growth can be attributed, in part, to an increase in feature advertising support and a five percent decline in unit price.

At SuperProfit Foods, Bargain Bubbles did not fare as well. It ranked fourth, down from third a year ago. Bargain Bubbles was significantly underdeveloped, with the retailer being responsible for only 11.6 percent of the brand's total market dollar volume. This compares with SuperProfit Foods' 18.3 percent share of market ACV and 15.9 percent share of shampoo category sales (see chart 3.9).

Although Bargain Bubbles lost 4.2 percent of its volume at SuperProfit Foods, this still was significantly less than the retailer's 19.6 percent volume loss in the shampoo category (see chart 3.9). Consequently, Bargain Bubbles gained 1.2 share points to reach a 7.3 share at SuperProfit Foods, which was still well below the 10.0 share Bargain Bubbles held in the market.

3.9 Major Brand Account/Market Review for Bargain Bubbles

13 weeks

	SuperProfit Foods (18.3% ACV)				Market					
	Dollar volume	% chg.	Dollar share	Share chg.	Dollar volume	% chg.	Dollar share	Share chg.	Acct. % of mkt.	Pt. chg.
Shampoo	780,567	-19.6	–	–	4,918,137	-3.5	–	–	15.9	-3.2
Bargain Bubbles	56,864	-4.2	7.3	1.2	490,164	17.4	10.0	1.8	11.6	-2.6
Clean & Soft	108,826	-12.4	13.9	1.1	621,171	-7.4	12.6	-0.5	17.5	-1.0
1st Impressions	77,672	-26.1	10.0	-0.9	448,013	-17.8	9.1	-1.6	17.3	-2.0
Mane Tame	64,446	29.6	8.3	3.1	308,605	44.1	6.3	2.1	20.9	-2.3
Silky Style	43,198	-20.5	5.5	-0.1	190,971	-19.9	3.9	-0.8	22.6	-0.2

Source: Nielsen Marketing Research, Sales Advisor

Manufacturers Looking for Ways to Turn Up the Volume

• • • • • • • • • • • • • • • •

During the latest quarter studied by Debonair, SuperProfit Foods battled category volume deficits on a weekly basis (see chart 3.10). During the quarter, there was only one week during which Bargain Bubbles achieved a share at SuperProfit Foods that was close to its 10.0 share of shampoo sales within the market. Promotion activity, including feature advertising, display and reduced retail

3.10 Product Comparison

13 Weeks
SuperProfit Foods
Bargain Bubbles—dollar share

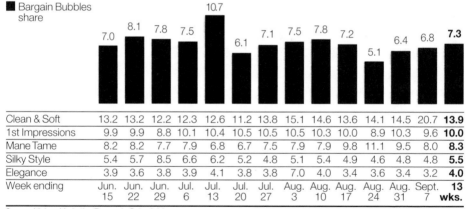

	1 wk.	1 wk.	1 wk.	1 wk.	1 wk.	1 wk.	1 wk.	1 wk.	1 wk.	1 wk.	1 wk.	1 wk.	1 wk.	**13 wks.**
Category volume	60243	61419	66743	52614	60103	62337	58425	57834	54481	59924	64086	59608	62748	**780567**
% chg. vs. year-ago	-31.4	-18.3	-14.6	-20.3	-14.8	-10.1	-15.1	-27.4	-21.2	-23.2	-22.6	-22.0	-9.3	**-19.6**
Clean & Soft	13.2	13.2	12.2	12.3	12.6	11.2	13.8	15.1	14.6	13.6	14.1	14.5	20.7	**13.9**
1st Impressions	9.9	9.9	8.8	10.1	10.4	10.5	10.5	10.5	10.3	10.0	8.9	10.3	9.6	**10.0**
Mane Tame	8.2	8.2	7.7	7.9	6.8	6.7	7.5	7.9	7.9	9.8	11.1	9.5	8.0	**8.3**
Silky Style	5.4	5.7	8.5	6.6	6.2	5.2	4.8	5.1	5.4	4.9	4.6	4.8	4.8	**5.5**
Elegance	3.9	3.6	3.8	3.9	4.1	3.8	3.8	7.0	4.0	3.4	3.6	3.4	3.2	**4.0**
Week ending	Jun. 15	Jun. 22	Jun. 29	Jul. 6	Jul. 13	Jul. 20	Jul. 27	Aug. 3	Aug. 10	Aug. 17	Aug. 24	Aug. 31	Sept. 7	**13 wks.**

Source: Nielsen Marketing Research, Sales Advisor

price, apparently contributed to Bargain Bubbles' higher one-week performance (see chart 3.11).

Using artificial intelligence once again, Debonair identifies three major factors contributing to Bargain Bubbles' performance at SuperProfit Foods.

• First, only 9.7 percent of Bargain Bubbles' dollar volume is sold on promotion within SuperProfit Foods, compared with 27.2 percent in the market (see chart 3.7), and 26.7 percent nationally. This indicates that SuperProfit Foods must promote Bargain Bubbles aggressively with a low price to move more product and to become more competitive within the market.

3.11 Product Profile

13 Weeks
SuperProfit Foods
Bargain Bubbles—dollar share

	1 wk.	1 wk.	1 wk.	1 wk.	1 wk.	1 wk.	1 wk.	1 wk.	1 wk.	1 wk.	1 wk.	1 wk.	1 wk.	**13 wks.**
Category volume	60243	61419	66743	52614	60103	62337	58425	57834	54481	59924	64086	59608	62748	**780567**
% chg. vs. year-ago	-31.4	-18.3	-14.6	-20.3	-14.8	-10.1	-15.1	-27.4	-21.2	-23.2	-22.6	-22.0	-9.3	**-19.6**

■ Bargain Bubbles share

Bar chart values: 7.0, 8.1, 7.8, 7.5, 10.7, 6.1, 7.1, 7.5, 7.8, 7.2, 5.1, 6.4, 6.8, **7.3**

Share change vs. year-ago	2.5	3.7	2.8	1.6	5.1	0.1	0.2	-10.3	2.9	3.2	1.1	1.6	0.9	**1.20**
% Promoted	0.0	0.0	0.0	0.0	85.7	0.0	0.0	0.0	0.0	0.0	0.0	0.0	0.0	**9.70**
% ACV major ad	0	0	0	0	81	0	0	0	0	0	0	0	0	**81.00**
% ACV display	0	0	0	0	21	0	0	0	0	0	0	0	0	**21.00**
Avg. price	1.39	1.39	1.41	1.56	1.06	1.57	1.55	1.56	1.56	1.57	1.55	1.56	1.56	**1.48**
Week ending	Jun. 15	Jun. 22	Jun. 29	Jul. 6	Jul. 13	Jul. 20	Jul. 27	Aug. 3	Aug. 10	Aug. 17	Aug. 24	Aug. 31	Sept. 7	**13 wks.**

Source: Nielsen Marketing Research, Sales Advisor

• • • • • • • • • • • • • • • • • • Second, Bargain Bubbles consistently sells for a higher price at SuperProfit Foods than elsewhere in the market, apparently because the item is a slow mover and the retailer is attempting to recover its investment. SuperProfit Foods prices Bargain Bubbles higher than elsewhere even when promoting the product. These pricing practices conflict with the brand's image.

• Third, SuperProfit Foods is carrying the wrong mix of Bargain Bubbles at the wrong stores. The highest-ranked item for Bargain Bubbles comes in at 27 even though Bargain Bubbles is the fourth-ranked brand at SuperProfit Foods and the second-ranked brand in the market. These data indicate that Debonair must look deeper than the total brand level to determine which product types and sizes contribute to the category's overall performance within individual store types.

Debonair knows that SuperProfit Foods is significantly underdeveloped in the shampoo category, accounting for only 15.9 percent of shampoo sales in the market while having an 18.3 percent share of market ACV. This 2.4 share difference represents an annual loss of $471,000 in shampoo category sales for SuperProfit Foods.

Using this knowledge, Debonair can develop a marketing and selling strategy that shows how Bargain Bubbles can help SuperProfit Foods improve shampoo category sales by modifying the brand's product mix, shelf space, promotions and pricing. The remaining steps within the category management process will provide the information that Debonair needs to determine the appropriate strategy.

2. Targeting Consumers

To develop a sound category management strategy, Debonair must have a thorough, broad-based understanding of how consumers purchase Bargain Bubbles and how they purchase all shampoo products. This will enable Debonair to match opportunities for Bargain Bubbles with those of the category on a store-by-store basis.

Through its analysis of demographic data, Debonair learns that the typical shampoo consumer comes from a family with at least one child, total income exceeding $30,000, and a female head of household between the ages of 18 and 44.

The typical Bargain Bubbles consumer also comes from a family with at least one child. However, more of the Bargain Bubbles buyers fall into lower-income segments than does the average shampoo buyer.

An examination of consumer purchase behavior in the shampoo category shows that deal purchasing of shampoo has increased in food stores, and that discounts offered by food retailers caused the average price paid per unit to decline by eight cents from the year-earlier period. (see chart 3.12).

While some consumers were likely to be "cherry-picking" shampoo promotions at food retailers, other shoppers apparently were shifting their category purchases to mass merchandisers to take advantage of a unit price 21 percent below that of food stores (see chart 3.12).

3.12 Shampoo—Deal Purchasing

Outlets	Avg. price paid		Percent of units on deal	
	Last year	This year	Last year	This year
Food ($4MM+)	$2.51	$2.43	40%	44%
Drug	$2.60	$2.66	11%	7%
Mass merchandiser	$1.97	$1.91	32%	28%

Source: Nielsen Marketing Research, Nielsen Household Services

Manufacturers Looking for Ways to Turn Up the Volume

During the most recent period, only 31 percent of shampoo buyers purchased the shampoo category either exclusively or primarily in food outlets—down from 36 percent during the prior year (see chart 3.13).

3.13 Shampoo Buyers by Outlet

	Last period	This period
Exclusive food	14%	12%
Loyal food	22%	19%
Outlet switchers	29%	31%
Loyal non-food	23%	25%
Exclusive non-food	12%	13%

Source: Nielsen Marketing Research, Nielsen Household Services

Based on this information, Debonair concludes that lower prices caused shampoo buyers to shift their outlet preference for the shampoo category away from food stores, and that food retailers will need to use the right assortment of products, pricing and promotional support to "re-attract" outlet switchers and to achieve their "fair share" of shampoo sales.

Customer Demographics Tell a Lot About a Person

Through an analysis of consumer purchase behavior for Bargain Bubbles, Debonair traces the sales increase for the brand to a slight increase in penetration and a larger increase in brand dollars per buyer (see chart 3.14).

3.14 Consumer Purchasing Patterns

Bargain Bubbles

	Penetration		Dollars/buyers	
	Last year	This year	Last year	This year
Bargain Bubbles	21%	22%	$3.02	$3.12
Clean & Soft	13%	15%	$7.99	$7.74

Source: Nielsen Marketing Research, Nielsen Household Services

3.15 Category Importance

	Bargain Bubbles	Clean & Soft
Category dollars per buyer	$17.33	$11.91
Percent of category volume from brand buyers	28%	16%

Source: Nielsen Marketing Research, Nielsen Household Services

Debonair also determines that although lower-priced Bargain Bubbles generates fewer brand dollars per buyer than the premium-priced Clean & Soft, consumer analysis shows that the Bargain Bubbles buyers are among the heaviest purchasers in the shampoo category. They spend $5.42 more per year on shampoo than Clean & Soft purchasers and account for 28 percent of the category's sales (see chart 3.15).

Based on this information, Debonair concludes that Bargain Bubbles is important to any retailer's product mix, and increased support from a food retailer would be justified in an attempt to re-attract consumers switching their purchases to non-food outlets.

With a 22 percent annual penetration rate among all households, Bargain Bubbles has the largest buyer base in the category (see chart 3.16). The brand's penetration rate among consumers buying

3.16 Brand Penetration Rates

Among:	Bargain Bubbles	Clean & Soft
All households	22%	15%
Exclusive/loyal non-food	28%	13%
Outlet switchers	25%	8%
Exclusive/loyal food	12%	24%

Source: Nielsen Marketing Research, Nielsen Household Services

Manufacturers Looking for Ways to Turn Up the Volume

• • • • • • • • • • • • • • • •

shampoo in non-food outlets is even higher—at 28 percent of the exclusive/loyal non-food buyers and 25 percent of outlet switchers.

By carrying and supporting Bargain Bubbles, a retailer will be merchandising a brand that has a larger group of consumers, and a more important group to category sales, than does premium-priced Clean & Soft.

Seeking to protect and build its brand franchise and increase its profitability, Debonair recognizes that its strategy should be to increase Bargain Bubbles' penetration rate within food outlets. As part of this strategy, the company decides to direct advertising at current Bargain Bubbles customers and competitive-brand buyers, and to improve the pricing, promotion and product mix for Bargain Bubbles at food retail chains where it is underperforming.

SuperProfit Foods is one of those chains. Consumer analysis reveals that heavy shampoo buyers and loyal Bargain Bubbles buyers are purchasing their shampoo somewhere besides SuperProfit Foods. The manufacturer sees an opportunity to help the chain attract shampoo buyers to its stores, while also protecting and building the Bargain Bubbles franchise.

Debonair knows that SuperProfit Foods' objective is to maximize the shampoo category's potential at each of its stores. To do this, the chain's category manager identifies "clusters" of consumers living in its trading areas and their shampoo purchasing behavior. Through consumer analysis, he learns that demographic characteristics such as income strongly influence shampoo purchases.

Using this knowledge, the category manager segments SuperProfit Foods stores into three types for the shampoo category—Upscale Affluent, Middle Income Families, and Inner City—based on the concentration of "clusters" in each store's trading area and their shampoo purchasing behavior. He then customizes the shampoo assortment, shelf space, inventory, and merchandising for each store type to meet consumer needs. Let's take a closer look at the characteristics of consumers at SuperProfit Foods' three target store types.

Members of Target Group 1, Upscale Affluent, include Suburban and Urban Professionals, as well as White-Collar Empty Nesters. A typical Group 1 consumer might drive an imported luxury car, downhill ski, play tennis and racquetball, and have a passport.

Debonair discovers that although SuperProfit Foods attracts a higher-than-expected percentage of Upscale Affluent consumers, they are not the heaviest buyers of shampoo and are not heavy buyers of Bargain Bubbles. The manufacturer develops a strategy for SuperProfit Foods' Upscale Affluent stores that calls for limiting the variety of Bargain Bubbles to only the best-selling items carrying a higher price, and increasing the variety of its upscale brand, Elegance.

Because Bargain Bubbles is a budget brand whose buyers skew toward middle-income households, the Middle Income Families stores of SuperProfit Foods offer greater potential for Bargain Bubbles sales than do the Upscale Affluent and Inner City stores. Target Group 2, Middle Income Families, emerges as a strong leverage point for Debonair. The group consists of White-Collar Families, Blue-Collar Families and Two-Income Households With Children. Typical Group 2 consumers often own a camper trailer, devote attention to lawn care, and frequent different types of restaurants than Group 1 consumers. They also might downhill ski, play racquetball, or go bowling.

Target Group 1

Manufacturers Looking for Ways to Turn Up the Volume

Further analysis of consumer data shows clear lifestyle distinctions between the Blue-Collar Families and White-Collar Families/Two-Income Households With Children components of Target Group 2. Blue-Collar Families are big users of contact lenses and in-home health-care services. They also often own a truck, listen to country music radio, enjoy hunting, and frequent fast-food restaurants and mass-merchandiser stores (see chart 3.17). Many of these households are headed by someone who does not have a high school diploma, and many have annual incomes of less than $15,000.

3.17 Lifestyles

Blue-Collar Families

Index

Index	
217	Wear contact lenses
217	Used in-home health care services
146	Number of days adults went hunting in last 12 months
142	Listen to country music radio
141	Education: less than high school graduate
139	Shop at Southern Supermarkets
136	Visit Hardees
133	Household owns Chevrolet truck
130	Adults shopped at Super Discount Mart last 3 months
129	Household owns Ford truck
128	Buy Peak antifreeze
128	Household income under $15,000
127	Adult drives compact/other pick-up truck
127	Visit Bonanza
127	Household owns medium dog (26-50 lbs.)
126	Occupation: other (blue collar) employed
126	Own rifle/shotgun for hunting
121	Visit Long John Silver
119	Use mail order for film processing
119	Visit Ponderosa Steak House

Source: Nielsen Marketing Research, ClusterPLUS, Nielsen Household Services, S.M.R.B.

White-Collar Families and Two-Income Households
With Children, by contrast, often own a dishwasher
and garbage disposal, lease a car, shop at food
stores and eat at national restaurant chains. Many
also spend money on home furnishings, own a personal computer and have an annual income of
$45,000 or more (see chart 3.18).

3.18 Lifestyles

White-Collar Families, 2-Income Households With Children

Index

152	Shop at High End Foods Supermarkets
147	Shop at Everyday Supermarkets
147	Amount spent by households for bedroom furniture last year (000)
145	Shop at The Best Stores
144	Household owns garbage disposal
143	Household owns dishwasher (automatic built-in)
142	Household owns truck mounted/towable camper
141	Own racquetball racquet
140	Household owns Honda car
140	Drive car leased by household
140	Visit TGI Friday's
139	No. dishloads done with auto dish detergent by households last week
137	No. packs of other still film used by adults last 12 months.
134	Visited gambling casino in last 12 months.
134	Amount spent by households for wall paper last year (000)
134	No. days adults went overnight camping in last 12 months.
134	Household income $45,000+
133	Household owns home/personal computer
133	Visit Fuddrucker's
133	Amount spent by households on wall/wall carpet–room size rug last year (000)

Source: Nielsen Marketing Research, ClusterPLUS, Nielsen Household Services, S.M.R.B.

Chapter 3

Manufacturers Looking for Ways to Turn Up the Volume

SuperProfit Foods is not attracting its fair share of Target Group 2 consumers from its trade area, yet they are heavy shampoo buyers, and their tendency to purchase Bargain Bubbles is above average (see chart 3.19). Because Bargain Bubbles sells well when promoted and is heavily promoted in this market as well as others, Debonair concludes that SuperProfit Foods needs to promote the brand more aggressively with an eye-catching price. The manufacturer decides that its strategy for the Middle Income Families stores will be to carry a full variety of items and maintain an everyday low price.

3.19 SuperProfit Foods (SPF)

Middle Income Families (Target Group 2)

Types of households	Distrib'n of households within SPF trade areas	Distrib'n of households shopping in SPF stores	Shampoo index	B.B.'s index
White-Collar Families	10.1%	8.5%	116	110
2-Income W/Children	11.2%	7.8%	116	128
Blue-Collar Families	18.2%	18.4%	121	103

Source: Nielsen Marketing Research, ClusterPLUS, Nielsen Household Services

In addition to providing the right price, promotions and merchandising, Debonair can use advertising to help SuperProfit Foods attract loyal Bargain Bubbles buyers into its stores. To target its advertising for Bargain Bubbles, Debonair examines the media preferences of the three subgroups that comprise Target Group 2.

The company learns that White-Collar Families and Two-Income Households With Children exhibit a preference for magazine, newspaper, outdoor and radio advertising. Members of these groups often read women's magazines, such as *Ladies Home Journal* and *Good Housekeeping*; news magazines, such as *U.S. News & World Report* and *Newsweek*; and outdoor or sports magazines, such as

Field & Stream and *Sports Illustrated*. They're most likely to listen to variety, religious, rock, adult contemporary and classical music stations.

Debonair discovers sharply different media preferences among the Blue-Collar Families in Target Group 2. They clearly prefer television over other media. Knowing this, Debonair can access data that indicate which television dayparts are most likely to attract Blue-Collar Families, whether they watch network, cable or local TV stations, and which programs are their favorites. The company discovers that prime-time network TV programs, including "Unsolved Mysteries," "America's Funniest Home Videos," "America's Funniest People" and "Rescue: 911," draw much higher percentages of viewers among Blue-Collar Families than they do among the population in general.

Using this media-preference knowledge, Debonair can develop advertising strategies customized for the three major subgroups that comprise Target Group 2.

Target Group 3, Inner City, is about 30 percent less likely to purchase shampoo and Bargain Bubbles than is the average consumer, making this group a less attractive target for Debonair.

National Advertising Creates National Benefits

By analyzing data on demographics, purchase behavior, promotion response, and other variables, Debonair becomes the category expert in identifying target groups of consumers.

Armed with all of this intelligence, Debonair's team sales leader plans to demonstrate during an upcoming presentation at SuperProfit Foods how Debonair's brands can help the chain attract more customers to its stores and improve category

• • • • • • • • • • • • • • •

volume and profits. By matching profiles of the chain's store trading areas with profiles of Bargain Bubbles and Elegance, the team sales leader plans to recommend targeted marketing strategies that will benefit both the retailer and Debonair's brands.

At the same time, he will tell the retailer that Debonair plans to advertise Bargain Bubbles through those advertising mediums that provide the greatest opportunity for reaching Bargain Bubbles' target consumers. Like many manufacturers, Debonair is now allocating more dollars to promotions and fewer dollars to advertising, so the company wants to maximize its Bargain Bubbles advertising investment by ensuring that its ads are well-targeted and efficient. It therefore targets White-Collar Families and Two-Income Households With Children with magazine, newspaper, and radio advertising, and it targets Blue-Collar Families with television advertising. The advertising will be designed to build brand equity by reinforcing the Bargain Bubbles message among current buyers of the brand, and by luring buyers of competitive brands. Debonair's team sales leader intends to emphasize to SuperProfit Foods that the chain will realize an indirect benefit locally from Debonair's national advertising. This will be especially true at the retailer's Middle Income Families stores, particularly if the retailer features Bargain Bubbles prominently in those locations.

Product-mix, pricing, promotion and shelf-space management strategies, of course, always must be developed with target customers in mind. In this case, Debonair is most interested in targeting the White-Collar Families, Blue-Collar Families and Two-Income Households With Children that comprise consumerTarget Group 2. It uses a demographic mapping program to identify the SuperProfit Foods stores with high concentrations of shoppers from these groups, and will target its new merchandising strategies to these stores (see chart 3.20).

3.20 SuperProfit Foods Trading Areas

Stores targeted for price/promotion/merchandising strategies for Target Group 2

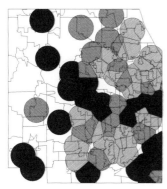

Store Rank
- ■ High
- ▨ Medium
- ☐ Low

Source: Nielsen Marketing Research, CONQUEST, ScorPLUS, Nielsen Household Services

By prioritizing marketing and merchandising opportunities on an individual-store basis for more efficient and effective sales coverage, Debonair has taken a major step toward forming a strategic alliance with SuperProfit Foods. In the next step of category management, Debonair's team sales leader will develop the appropriate product mix, pricing, promotion and shelf-space strategies to help SuperProfit Foods' Middle Income Families stores attract loyal Bargain Bubbles buyers who are shopping elsewhere.

Chapter 3

Manufacturers Looking for Ways to Turn Up the Volume

• • • • • • • • • • • • • • • • • ### 3. Planning Merchandising

Using software modeling programs that analyze product mix from the standpoint of volume and profitability, Debonair determines that its product mix at SuperProfit Foods could be improved. It learns that the chain does not handle five of Debonair's shampoo products, which together generated unit sales of 28,219 during a recent 13-week period in the market studied, for a market share of 1.5. Of these products, the leading item was the 16-oz. size of Bargain Bubbles (see chart 3.21).

3.21 Items Not Handled Report for Debonair, Inc. in SuperProfit Foods

13 weeks

	Rem. mkt. unit sales	Rem. mkt. unit share	Rem. mkt. sales per $MM ACV	Rem. market %SS	Acct. unit sales potential	Potential rank in acct.@ 100%SS
Total category	1,827,599		649.8	100		
Bargain Bubbles VIT REG Lq. 16 oz.	11,038	0.6	20.4	24	9,563	7
Bargain Bubbles RS REG. Lq. 16 oz.	5,475	0.3	8.7	28	4,089	58
Silky Style S&C. X-B Lq. 10 oz.	4,649	0.3	7.4	28	3,451	77
Silky Style S&C. Lq. 15 oz.	3,800	0.2	6.6	26	3,105	96
Elegance X-B Lq. 15 oz.	3,257	0.2	7.0	22	3,274	85
Total	28,219	1.5				

Source: Nielsen Marketing Research, Sales Advisor

Debonair models a number of potential product mix scenarios and settles on one that calls for adding the 16-oz. size of Bargain Bubbles and several other brands, including competitors', to the shampoo category at SuperProfit Foods stores, while delisting the 12 oz. size of Bargain Bubbles, along with several other items. Debonair calculates that if the chain follows this recommendation, it could realize a category unit volume gain of 90,537 over a 13-week period. Assuming a gross margin of 25 percent, the potential net profit for the chain would total $22,632 (see chart 3.22).

In comparing category pricing data for the market and for SuperProfit Foods, Debonair determines that the chain's prices, on average, are 31 cents higher for the category, and 44 cents higher for

3.22 Distribution Opportunity—SuperProfit Foods

13 weeks	Chain Dist.	$/MM ACV	Projected Volume	Net Profit
Authorize distribution				
1st DF N/D Lq. 18 oz.		37.7	17,650	4,412
Mn. Tm. N Lq. 15 oz.		30.4	14,236	3,559
N. Hr. N/O Lq. 10 oz.		28.0	13,106	3,276
S. St. S&C X-B Lq. 15 oz.		22.9	10,710	2,677
B. B. REG Lq. 16 oz.		22.3	10,447	2,612
S. St. S&C Lq. 10 oz.		18.8	8,793	2,198
Elg. X-B Lq. 15 oz.		15.9	7,448	1,862
T.P. CD Lq. 32 oz.		15.1	7,053	1,763
L. Mn. MSTG Lq. 18 oz.		14.9	6,995	1,749
Cl. & S. O Lq. T15 oz.		14.9	6,990	1,747
Subtotal			103,428	25,855
De-list				
D. C N X-B Lq. 11 oz.	28	4.8	654	163
Nt. Cr. N Lq. 15 oz.	54	5.2	1,323	331
B. B. X-B Lq. 12 oz.	54	5.2	1,322	331
Nt. Cr. X-B Lq. 15 oz.	58	5.3	1,448	362
L. Mn. DF X-B Lq. 18 oz.	39	5.3	995	249
Shn. H Lq. 15 oz.	27	5.7	748	187
L. Mn. O Lq. 15 oz.	54	5.8	1,454	364
L. Mn. D Lq. 15 oz.	58	5.8	1,585	396
Trs. ND Lq. 15 oz.	55	5.8	1,519	380
B. B. ND Lq. 12 oz.	66	6.0	1,842	460
Subtotal			12,890	3,223
Total			**90,537**	**22,632**

Source: Nielsen Marketing Research, Sales Advisor

Chapter 3

Manufacturers Looking for Ways to Turn Up the Volume

• • • • • • • • • • • • • • • •

Debonair's products during a recent 13-week period. Using software applications, Debonair projects the results of a variety of pricing scenarios for the category and its products, leading the manufacturer to conclude that by implementing a lower-price strategy for Debonair's products, SuperProfit Foods can increase both volume and profitability for the category (see chart 3.23).

3.23 Price Comparison for Debonair, Inc.

13 weeks
Unit price SuperProfit Foods vs. market

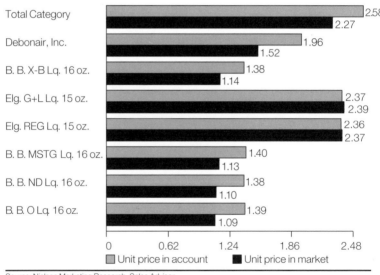

Source: Nielsen Marketing Research, Sales Advisor

State-of-the-art modeling allows Debonair to quickly analyze various merchandising strategies. The manufacturer looks at sales multipliers at a 20 percent discount across promotion conditions for Bargain Bubbles, as compared with Stylish, Clean & Soft and Mane Tame (see chart 3.24). The multipliers represent the number of base weeks of volume that will be sold during the deal week.

146

3.24 Comparison of Competitive Items

SuperProfit Foods
Shampoo—unit basis
(20 percent deal discount)

Sales multiplier

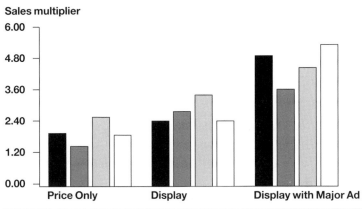

Brand item	Base share	Deal price	Price only	Display	Display w/ major ad
■ Bargain Bubbles	13.99	1.19	2.00	2.46	4.91
■ Stylish	3.14	2.09	1.51	2.82	3.65
▨ Clean & Soft	5.87	2.89	2.61	3.44	4.46
☐ Mane Tame	3.64	2.89	1.93	2.46	5.33

Source: Nielsen Marketing Research, Category Manager

It is apparent that all brands get a significant increase in sales if a display and major ad are used, rather than just a display. With a display and major ad, Bargain Bubbles has a stronger response rate than Stylish or Clean & Soft. Bargain Bubbles' sales will increase by 4.91 times normal movement, while Stylish will sell only 3.65 times its base sales, and Clean & Soft, 4.46 times its base sales. In addition, Bargain Bubbles has a smaller sales multiplier than Mane Tame, but Mane Tame's base share is significantly smaller than Bargain Bubbles'—3.64 versus 13.99.

Debonair next analyzes the category-wide impact of brand promotions. Assessing absolute increases in sales, instead of relative increases, will take into

Manufacturers Looking for Ways to Turn Up the Volume

account the base shares. The manufacturer looks at incremental cases for both the brand and the category, with about a 20 percent price cut accompanying a display and major ad (see chart 3.25). Clearly, Bargain Bubbles has the greatest incremental brand and category sales.

But the difference between the brand and category incremental sales is the amount that is cannibalized from the category's other brands. When Bargain Bubbles is promoted, 457.39 units are cannibalized from other brands. That means Bargain Bubbles has a 5 percent cannibalization rate. A further look enables Debonair to determine that Bargain Bubbles' cannibalization rate is much less than the rates of cannibalization for Stylish, Clean & Soft, and Mane Tame—which range from 13 to 28 percent (see chart 3.25).

3.25 Incremental Sales and Category Profit

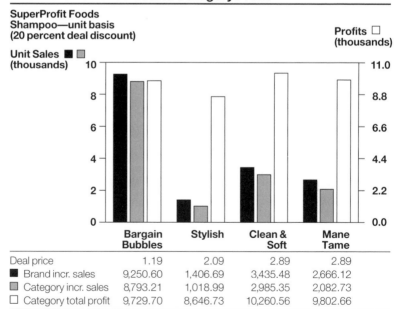

SuperProfit Foods
Shampoo—unit basis
(20 percent deal discount)

Profits □
(thousands)

Unit Sales ■ ▨
(thousands)

	Bargain Bubbles	Stylish	Clean & Soft	Mane Tame
Deal price	1.19	2.09	2.89	2.89
■ Brand incr. sales	9,250.60	1,406.69	3,435.48	2,666.12
▨ Category incr. sales	8,793.21	1,018.99	2,985.35	2,082.73
□ Category total profit	9,729.70	8,646.73	10,260.56	9,802.66

Source: Nielsen Marketing Research, Category Manager

Therefore, from a volume standpoint, with all other factors being equal, Debonair concludes that it is in SuperProfit Foods' best interest to promote Bargain Bubbles. Given the margins involved on these brands, it is more profitable, when considering retail category profit, to promote Bargain Bubbles than to promote Stylish (see chart 3.25). And Bargain Bubbles is only slightly less profitable than Clean & Soft and Mane Tame.

Once a decision is made to promote a brand, the manufacturer and retailer should determine together the optimal merchandising strategy. A model compares profitability for both partners at two different price points—$1.39 and $1.09—using a display and major ad. By reducing the price 30 cents, with all else equal, Debonair will shift from negative incremental profit of $594.00 to positive incremental profit of $2,244.49, an increase of $2,838.49 (see chart 3.26). In addition, the number of cases sold for the deal week will jump by 55 percent.

3.26 Plan and Calculate Deal Profitability

SuperProfit Foods–shampoo

Bargain Bubbles

Average shelf retail/unit	$1.51	
Promotion	Display w/major ad	

SuperProfit Foods Deal retail/unit	$1.39	$1.09	Debonair, Inc. Deal retail/unit	$1.39	$1.09
Baseline equivalized category case sales	16,925.96	16,925.96	Total cases bought	8,094.02	12,537.85
			Net deal dollars	3,689.32	7,910.46
Deal week equivalized category case sales	22,485.26	26,483.75	Total mfg. and distribution cost	2,428.21	3,761.36
Incremental category cases	5,559.30	9,557.79	Net corporate profit (loss)	1,261.11	4,149.60
Total category profit	14,599.97	12,644.75	Total base profit	1,855.11	1,855.11
Total category base profit	8,109.10	8,109.10	Incremental corp. profit (loss)	(594.00)	2,244.49
Incremental deal profit	6,490.87	4,535.65			

Source: Nielsen Marketing Research, Category Manager

Manufacturers Looking for Ways to Turn Up the Volume

As might be expected, it will not be as profitable for the retailer if the price is reduced to $1.09. SuperProfit Foods' incremental profit will drop from $6,490.87 to $4,535.65, a loss of $1,955.22 (see chart 3.26). However, Debonair's gain is greater than SuperProfit Foods' loss. Therefore, Debonair can compensate SuperProfit Foods for its loss of $1,955.22 by reducing their cost, and still make a profit of $883.27. Thus, there is a strategy that will increase sales, maintain retail profit and boost the manufacturer's gains.

Turning its attention to shelf space, Debonair recognizes that if SuperProfit Foods is to capitalize on the potential of Bargain Bubbles to attract buyers into its stores, the brand must occupy a more prominent position on the shelf. The planogram currently used by the retailer positions Bargain Bubbles along the bottom shelf. After deciding that Bargain Bubbles should be positioned horizontally at eye level, Debonair uses a shelf-space management software program to determine the linear space it will recommend for the brand based on its contribution to category volume and profits (see chart 3.27).

3.27 Sales Analysis for Debonair, Inc.

	NOF	Sales	Sales %	Sales/ LIN	Profit
Total Silky Style	8	$2,850.90	6.3	10,438.59	$916.37
Total Elegance	9	$1,985.31	4.4	5,334.84	$490.20
Total Bargain Bubbles	28	$1,983.76	4.5	5,668.92	$374.09
Total Debonair	**45**	**$6,819.97**	**15.2**	**21,442.34**	**$1,780.66**

Source: Nielsen Marketing Research, SPACEMAN

After developing the details of its merchandising strategies and the advertising programs it plans to support them, Debonair is ready to put them to the test.

4. Implementing Strategy

Debonair's team sales leader meets with the shampoo category buyer from SuperProfit Foods and reviews his analysis of the category, brand and consumer purchasing patterns. The team sales leader then presents the retailer with the product-mix, pricing, promotion and shelf-space strategies that he is recommending to help the chain attract more customers to its stores and improve category volume and profits.

He uses the customized demographic map to show which SuperProfit Foods stores have the highest concentrations of target customers and therefore should implement the targeted strategies (see chart 3.20).

To support his recommendations, the team sales leader uses appropriate charts and tables from his analyses. To illustrate the impact of adding certain products to the category and delisting others, he presents customized tables that name the products, project the volume and net profit each is likely to generate during a certain period, and project the change in category volume and profit likely to result from Debonair's recommendations (see chart 3.22).

Manufacturers Looking for Ways to Turn Up the Volume

• • • • • • • • • • • • • • • • He also presents customized planograms showing exactly how and where each product should be displayed on the shelf (see chart 3.28).

In addition, he uses tables produced by state-of-the-art modeling programs to show the buyer how pricing and promotion strategies will affect the volume and profitability of individual brands and the category as a whole (see chart 3.26). And he describes Debonair's national advertising strategy, using lists that relate particular types of advertising to specific target groups, and explaining how the targeted ads will benefit SuperProfit Foods' stores indirectly, especially if the stores support Bargain Bubbles with the right pricing, promotions and shelf space.

3.28 Shampoo Planogram for Middle Income Families Stores

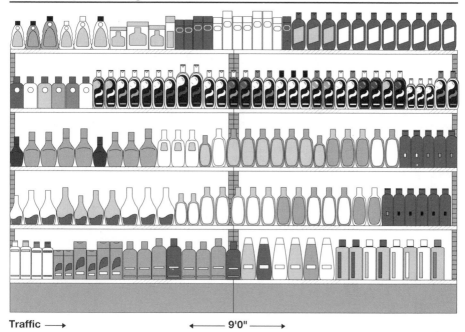

Traffic ⟶   ←——— 9'0" ———→

Source: Nielsen Marketing Research, SPACEMAN

Although the presentation is a major event in the relationship between Debonair and SuperProfit Foods, it is just a small piece of their ongoing relationship. Through presentations such as this one, Debonair establishes itself as a respected authority on the shampoo category, and enjoys a continuing dialogue with SuperProfit Foods about how to improve category volume and profits.

5. Evaluating Results

After implementing its shampoo marketing and merchandising strategies at SuperProfit Foods, Debonair begins the fifth stage of the category management process, evaluating results.

The key question Debonair wants to answer, of course, is: "Were our recommended product-mix, pricing, promotion and shelf-space management strategies effective in building share for Bargain Bubbles and in driving up shampoo category volume and profits for SuperProfit Foods?"

Debonair also wants to know how specifically its Bargain Bubbles strategies contributed to the category's performance. Did they, for example, cause an increase in the number of shampoo buyers? Or did the same number of buyers purchase more shampoo than usual on each shopping trip?

In addition, the manufacturer wants to determine whether Bargain Bubbles helped SuperProfit Foods attract shampoo buyers to its stores from competitors' stores, and, if it did, which types of competitors—other food stores, mass merchandisers or drug stores—lost sales as a result.

• • • • • • • • • • • • • • • •   Other questions Debonair asks include:

- Were our sales and profit estimates for SuperProfit Foods on target?

- What was the incremental volume generated for Bargain Bubbles by displays, ads and price reductions?

- Did the productivity of items in the category improve?

- Did we meet our objectives for sales, profit and return on investment?

- What type of strategies did competing brands pursue? How successful were they?

- Did we optimize shelf-space and inventory requirements? Or were there problems with product mix, facings, out-of-stocks and overstocks?

- How has Debonair's relationship with SuperProfit Foods developed?

Using a variety of software applications that combine scanning, causal and other information, Debonair is able to answer these questions and others through continual monitoring of the performance of the shampoo category in general and Bargain Bubbles in particular.

The manufacturer not only shares this information with SuperProfit Foods, but also quickly recommends new or modified strategies in response to problems or opportunities that arise within the category. This type of feedback contributes to a strong, long-term relationship between SuperProfit Foods and Debonair, and enhances both parties' chances of success in the shampoo category. Because in the long run, what's good for SuperProfit Foods is good for Debonair.

CHAPTER 4

· ·

**Cloudy Marketplace
Makes Future of
Category Manage-
ment Clear**

Cloudy Marketplace Makes Future of Category Management Clear

• • • • • • • • • • • • • • • The advances in technology, applications and information that have made category management possible soon will be supplanted by a new wave of innovation.

It not only will enhance the process of category management, but also will cause additional restructuring among manufacturers and retailers and redefine their relationship even further.

These changes will create additional challenges for people involved in category management programs. They will face new responsibilities requiring multiple skills in an increasingly fast-paced business environment.

What will drive the changes that lie ahead?

The key factors will be intensifying competition among retailers and the continued shifting of manu-facturers' market-share war to the store level.

As the lines separating retail trade channels become murkier, retailers will strive even harder to differentiate themselves, leading to increased niche marketing within each channel.

With more and more shoppers making their brand purchase decisions in the store, manufacturers will want to align their marketing efforts with retailers' niche strategies to enhance brand performance.

These trends will spur advances in technology, applications and information that will:

• Allow retailers at the headquarters level to cus-tomize merchandising plans for individual stores—instead of groups of stores—as well as for individual categories within each store.

• Enable manufacturers to monitor more closely brand performance within individual trade channels. This capability will help manufacturers develop cus-tomized marketing and merchandising strategies by category for each channel.

- Provide customer-specific purchase data. This will shift the focus of category management from the category-wide impact of individual products to their effect on the total customer transaction, overall store performance, and overall company performance.

- Put real-time information, customized by job function, at the fingertips of managers at multiple levels and in various departments within retailer and manufacturer organizations.

- Allow the use of artificial intelligence to manage and analyze an increasing data flow and to speed merchandising decisions.

POS Systems Getting Right to the Point

Although today's POS scanning systems are a far cry from the cash registers of yesteryear, the POS systems of tomorrow will make current technology appear simplistic by comparison.

The systems now in place are designed to allow retailers to make day-to-day replenishment and financial decisions, not merchandising decisions. Retailers can tell how many of which items were sold, when and where they were sold, and for what price. But scanning data reveals nothing about the nature of individual transactions and the causal factors that shape shoppers' purchase decisions.

In the future, POS systems not only will generate cleaner and more accurate data, but also will provide an in-depth look at how individual customers shop each store. These systems will feature stringently designed, relational databases that will yield data on the number of units sold as well as:

- The average number of items in a market-basket transaction.
- The average value of a market-basket transaction.
- The number of baskets containing a specific category.
- The percentage of total market-basket value accounted for by each category.
- How one item's sales affect sales of other items in the same category.

These new systems will allow retailers to determine when and how data are aggregated, which will facilitate merchandising decisions. Retailers will be able to produce time-oriented tables, including ones with data on weekly store performance; event-oriented tables, linking promotional events to specific products and time periods; item family tables, connecting UPCs to brands, manufacturers, categories and departments; market-basket tables, tying item performance to customer transaction data; and customer purchase tables, which relate customer profiles to data contained in the other tables.

These customer-specific data will go far beyond today's basic scanning data, enhancing retailers' and manufacturers' knowledge about the demographics, lifestyles and purchase behavior of individual consumers. The data will provide the answers to questions such as:

- Who bought the item?
- How many did the customer buy?
- When did the customer buy it?
- What else did the customer purchase?
- Is this customer a repeat buyer over time?
- Why did the customer buy the item? Was it on sale? Was it on display?
- Who is or isn't shopping a category?

By analyzing the answers to such questions, retailers will get a clear picture of the customer demographics and purchase behavior of individual stores and specific categories within those stores. This knowledge will lead to the development of store-specific merchandising programs, including customized strategies for individual categories. Decisions about pricing, promotions, product mix and product placement will be fine-tuned based on local customers' lifestyles and preferences. And a better understanding of brand trial and switching, consumer segment marketing, cherrypicking and lost customers will emerge.

The availability of transaction-specific data will shift the focus of category management from what an item or brand does for a category to what it does for the store and how it affects the entire customer transaction. For example, decisions on which items to promote will be based on the projected impact on total store traffic and the average customer transaction, and not just on the projected impact on item or brand performance. Other important factors in merchandising decisions will include the preferences of the store's target consumers, the appeal of an item or brand to all store customers, the relationship of one category to another, and the impact on traffic within a department.

Expanded POS data capabilities will lead to increased use of knowledge-based technology systems—also known as artificial intelligence systems—to accomplish store-specific merchandising. These systems will enable retailers and manufacturers to harness the power of a POS data flow that could be as much as 400 to 500 times greater than it is today. Encoded with the knowledge and reasoning processes of individual users and other experts, an artificial-intelligence system will mimic human behavior as it automatically digests data and

• • • • • • • • • • • • • • • •

solves problems related to merchandising deci-sions. For example, it might discover relationships between items or brands to maximize promotions, or it might assess the impact of an item or brand on the total customer transaction.

Knowledge-based technology will simplify the multitude of additional decision-making tasks and details that will accompany the increased flow of POS data in the years ahead. By quickly handling routine but time-consuming thought processes, these systems will free managers to concentrate on planning, management and application of their creative thought processes to merchandising decisions. If the system can't perform up to pro-grammed expectations, it will alert the manager. For example, the system might not be able to recommend whether a store should carry a new product because the system lacks an understanding of the product and whether or not it would appeal to the store's customers.

Manufacturers Leveraging Niche Strengths

The explosion of POS data, including continued expansion of third-party databases containing household purchase data, and the increased use of scanning systems in trade channels other than food stores, will give manufacturers unprecedented insights into consumer purchase behavior and how it affects various trade channels.

Just as retailers will seek to differentiate themselves through niche marketing, manufacturers will look for trade-channel niches with strong potential for certain categories. Using POS and other data, they will be able to identify category sales shifts among trade channels and understand what's behind them. When they find the right niche for their brands, they will be able to leverage it with strategies customized by category for each trade channel.

Keeping track of what's happening within different trade channels in specific markets will become easier and quicker than ever, despite an ever-growing data stream. Software already is available that allows manufacturers to take a "workbench" approach to managing and analyzing market data, and the use of such applications will become more widespread. The software, which integrates scanning data, internal data and data from external databases, can be customized by job function to deliver slices of relevant data quickly to the user, enhancing decision-making capabilities. This type of application will increase access to market data among non-marketing functions within manufacturers' organizations, including sales, finance and top management.

In the future, workbench applications also will become available to retailers, allowing them to drill down quickly through layers of market data to arrive at store-specific data. A store manager, for example, might use such applications to analyze the performance of major departments, categories or brands, and to compare market-basket transactions at his store with those at others.

Tomorrow's Organizational Structures Will Provide Flexible Support

While enhancing retailers' and manufacturers' ability to view the market from both a macrocosmic and microcosmic perspective, continued advances in technology, applications and information will lead to further changes within manufacturer and retailer organizations practicing category management.

Cloudy Marketplace Makes Future of Category Management Clear

• • • • • • • • • • • • • • • •   The structures of such organizations will be varied and dynamic, as companies learn more about the intricacies of the process and adjust to the changes around them. Newcomers to the process will benefit from the experiences of today's category management leaders, and as a result, implementation time periods for the process will shrink from their current level of three to five years.

Inevitably, the implementation and evolution of category management at a company causes a certain amount of employee turnover, because the process requires significant cultural and personal adaptations that prove difficult or impossible for some people to make. It demands, for example, that managers—particularly category managers— be more free-standing and capable of making objective decisions quickly.

As the focus of category management shifts to the impact of categories on market-basket transactions, departments and stores, the process will become even more demanding. To practice category management successfully, category managers will have to see the forest *and* the trees. They not only will have to be experts on the workings of individual categories, but they also will have to be able to relate category performance to the big picture—on a storewide, companywide and marketwide basis.

When buyer and seller meet in the future, each will have to understand not only the purchase behavior of demographic cluster groups but also the shopping habits of customers at specific stores. The category manager also will have to consider a variety of other issues. For example, when a person buys a product from a certain category, what other items are in his basket? How important is a category to the entire store?

These changes will mean that the lines between manufacturers' sales and marketing departments will blur even further, with sales taking on more of a marketing mentality and vice versa.

Responsible primarily for implementation and execution in the past, sales will work with marketing through the five stages of category management. Sales also will interact with other departments, such as MIS, research and finance, which will integrate and leverage internal data and syndicated data to support sales and marketing activities. At the same time, sales will be responsible for developing strong, long-term relationships with retail customers.

To handle these responsibilities effectively, sales managers will need strong analytical, logistical and communications skills. They will have to understand the objectives of retail accounts as well as their own company. And they will have to be knowledgeable and versatile enough to interact easily with a variety of departments within their company. At one moment, they might be huddling with marketing managers to identify market trends, and at the next, they might be talking with shipping/distribution managers about getting products to a customer faster.

Advances in technology, applications and information—including "workbench" applications and artificial intelligence—will enable sales managers to handle these additional duties efficiently by putting customized and actionable market data in their hands on a real-time basis with a minimum of manual work. But sales managers—as well as marketing managers and retail category managers—still will need technical skills to access necessary data quickly and to use it to its full potential.

Chapter 4

Cloudy Marketplace Makes Future of Category Management Clear

As sales becomes more involved in responsibilities formerly handled by marketing, marketing managers will concentrate more on building and managing brand franchises. They will focus on establishing brand images and cultivating them with creative advertising and promotion campaigns. They also will determine how new products might contribute to their overall effort to differentiate their brands from the rest of the pack.

This effort will require brand managers to understand the ebb and flow of business by category among retail trade channels and to identify niches with strong potential for their brands. To do so successfully, marketing managers will have to develop skills traditionally associated with sales. Specifically, they will have to understand the strategic objectives of retail customers in addition to the purchase behavior of shoppers.

The increased availability of actionable market data at all levels of manufacturers' organizations will foster interaction among various departments and the growth of "matrix management" structures, in which individuals not only rely on people outside their own departments, but in some cases also report on a dotted-line basis to non-department managers.

Strategic Alliances Will Focus on 'Win-Win' Results

Growing numbers of manufacturers and retailers with category management programs will form strategic alliances to manage the increased flow of market data better and to achieve their individual strategic objectives.

Under these alliances, manufacturers and retailers will share data resources as well as macrocosmic and microcosmic market knowledge and category insights. Each party will strive to advocate the other's strategic objectives and to cooperate in a joint effort to achieve them—so long as the effort produces a "win-win" result. Similar alliances will proliferate between manufacturers and retailers and third-party data suppliers.

The retailer-manufacturer alliances of tomorrow will be focused on the store, because that is where the product, the customer, the manufacturer's marketing plan and the retailer's marketing and merchandising plan will converge. Category management will create a common framework for these alliances, enabling retailers and manufacturers to develop empirically-based, mutually beneficial strategies for pushing more products out the front door.

With POS data and household purchase behavior data becoming more abundant and more sophisticated, manufacturers and retailers increasingly will fine-tune marketing and merchandising strategies based on individual customer transactions at specific stores.

But as important as the new wave of technology, applications and information will be to category management, strategic alliances and the development of precisely targeted strategies, it will not be the deciding factor in the fight for preeminence in the consumer packaged goods marketplace.

Selling products to consumers will remain a people business. People still will make the products. People will sell them into retail locations. People will select them and put them in their shopping baskets. People will pass the products over electronic scanners and accept payment from customers.

Cloudy Marketplace Makes Future of Category Management Clear

• • • • • • • • • • • • • • • •

And other people will analyze scanning data to help people understand why people shop the way they do.

Retailers and manufacturers must not lose sight of these simple facts as they ride the high-tech marketing wave of the future. In dealing with employees, trade partners and consumers, it will be the human touch—not computer-generated data—that wins the day.

The companies that can balance high-tech with a human touch, listening to and understanding customers as they customize and analyze market data, will be the ones that reap the full benefits of category management and emerge as the marketplace leaders of tomorrow.

APPENDIX A

Appendix

• • • • • • • • • • • • • • •

The Category Management
process described in this
book is a combination
of advanced software
tools and consulting.
The products used to
create the information
and charts in the case
study are listed here.

List of Products: Chapter 2—Retailers

Reviewing Category
Nielsen Highlights
SCAN❋FACT® PC for Retailers
SPACEMAN®
Consumer Marketing Applications
(Nielsen Household Services)

Targeting Consumers
Consumer Marketing Applications
(Nielsen Household Services)
Conquest®
ClusterPLUS®

Planning Merchandising
SCAN❋FACT® PC for Retailers
Nielsen Promotion Management System (PROMOMAN)
Nielsen Retail Price Simulator (PRICEMAN)
SPACEMAN®
Category Manager
Consumer Marketing Applications
(Nielsen Household Services)
ClusterPLUS®

Implementing Strategy
SPACEMAN®
Nielsen Retail Price Simulator (PRICEMAN)
Nielsen Promotion Management System (PROMOMAN)
ASTRO-SET™

Evaluating Results
SCAN❋FACT® PC for Retailers
Consumer Marketing Applications
(Nielsen Household Services)
Nielsen Retail Price Simulator (PRICEMAN)
Nielsen Promotion Management System (PROMOMAN)
SPACEMAN®

List of Products: Chapter 3—Manufacturers

Reviewing Category

Nielsen Highlights

Consumer Marketing Applications
(Nielsen Household Services)

Nielsen Spotlight®

Nielsen Sales Advisor®

Market/Retail Opportunity Reports

SPACEMAN®

Procision®

Targeting Consumers

Consumer Marketing Applications
(Nielsen Household Services)

Conquest®

ScorPLUS™

ClusterPLUS®

Planning Merchandising

Nielsen Sales Advisor®

Category Manager

SPACEMAN®

Consumer Marketing Applications
(Nielsen Household Services)

ClusterPLUS®

Implementing Strategy

Nielsen Sales Advisor®

Category Manager

SPACEMAN®

Evaluating Results

Nielsen Sales Advisor®

Nielsen Spotlight®

Consumer Marketing Applications
(Nielsen Household Services)

SPACEMAN®

Appendix

Appendix

INDEX

Index